KADIAN JOURNAL

A Father's Story

Thomas Harding

WILLIAM HEINEMANN: LONDON

Published by William Heinemann 2014

2 4 6 8 10 9 7 5 3 1

First published in Great Britain in 2014 by
William Heinemann
Random House, 20 Vauxhall Bridge Road,
London SW1V 2SA

www.randomhouse.co.uk

Addresses for companies within The Random House Group Limited can be found at:
www.randomhouse.co.uk/offices.htm

The Random House Group Limited Reg. No. 954009

A CIP catalogue record for this book
is available from the British Library

ISBN 9780434023011

The Random House Group Limited supports the Forest Stewardship Council® (FSC®), the leading international forest-certification organisation. Our books carrying the FSC label are printed on FSC®-certified paper. FSC is the only forest-certification scheme supported by the leading environmental organisations, including Greenpeace. Our paper procurement policy can be found at www.randomhouse.co.uk/environment

Typeset in FournierMT by Palimpsest Book Production Limited,
Falkirk, Stirlingshire

Printed and bound in Great Britain by Clays Ltd, St Ives PLC

The wintry garden lies unchanged,
The brook into the stream runs on,
But the deep-eyed Boy is gone.

'Threnody'
Ralph Waldo Emerson

It is not growing like a tree
In bulk, doth make Man better be;
Or standing long an oak, three hundred year,
To fall a log at last, dry, bald, and sere:
A lily of a day
Is fairer far in May,
Although it fall and die that night—
It was the plant and flower of Light
In small proportions we just beauties see;
And in short measures life may perfect be.

'The Noble Nature'
Ben Jonson

PART I

25 July 2012

We are cycling up a narrow country lane to the ridge at the top of the Downs. It is early evening. There is not a cloud in the sky. The air is soft and warm after a day of baking sun.

There are six of us: my twenty-one-year-old nephew Taylor, my sister Amanda and her friend Anne-Claire, my fourteen-year-old son Kadian, his school friend Rori, and me.

As Kadian climbs the hill I call from behind, encouraging him to practise his turning signals. He puts his right arm out and the bike wobbles in the same direction. 'You need to lean to the left when you signal right,' I shout from behind. 'Try it.' He does, and it is marginally better. When I tell him to do it again, he grunts in disgust and, pressing hard on his pedals, pulls away from me up the hill.

We are staying at my parents' house in Mildenhall, a village just outside Marlborough in Wiltshire. Our plan is to cycle ten miles west, to my uncle and aunt's thatched cottage, for a family dinner. The journey will take us up and across the Marlborough Downs, a chain of grassland chalk hills that separates the county of Oxfordshire in the north from Wiltshire in the south. Along its top runs an ancient footpath, known as the Ridgeway, and it is this that we intend to follow.

We continue our way up the lane and the vista opens. There is a field filled with golden wheat on our left. Another speckled with grazing sheep and Neolithic stones. Below us a grassy slope drops away to fields etched with terraces. The ringed mounds of ancient hill forts can be seen in the distance. The sun, sitting low in the sky, splashes amber light across the landscape.

'It is so beautiful here,' Kadian says as I pull up to him. 'It's so beautiful,' he repeats with a dreamy smile.

We wait for the others to catch up then head off the lane onto a stony track that descends gently down to a large stack of hay bales. The trail ends abruptly, which is strange. I look at my map, trying to figure out where we have gone wrong. Kadian cycles behind the hay and calls out, 'It's over here, the footpath is over here.'

Kadian goes first, and the rest of us follow. Soon we are riding along a narrow path through a tunnel of trees. Kadian, still in front, calls back, 'It's muddy, it's muddy,' in a not very believable but still funny northern accent.

The path opens into a broader track. It's a little gravelly, steeper. The gap between myself and Kadian widens. I notice this, the information sliding though my mind without traction as I grasp my brakes to slow my descent.

He's suddenly way ahead of me. A hundred feet perhaps. He must have gathered speed. And then there's a flash of a white van, moving fast from left to right, at the bottom of the slope. It shouldn't be there. And the van hits Kadian. Driving him away from view, away from me.

Moments later I'm at the road. I drop my bike to the ground. I'm screaming before I see him. He's lying face down on the side of the road, near the white line. His head is tilted to the left; there is a small pool of blood by his mouth. I can't see his bike. He is still. Absolutely still. He doesn't look like Kadian any more. He looks vacant. He looks like he is six or seven years old. But what strikes me the most, more than the blood, or the lack of movement, are his eyes. His pupils are dilated unnaturally wide. I know he's gone. I know he is dead. I know that I have lost my son. My Kadian.

This is real. This is happening. I can't believe it. I'm crouching a few feet from him. Wailing. My head in my hands. And wailing. No. No. No. I don't want to touch him. I don't want to cradle him in my arms. I want to roll back time. I am both in my body, rocking, howling, and high above, looking down on this dreadful scene, feeling oddly sorry for the father who has just lost his son, suddenly, tragically.

I realise that this is the A4, the road running from Marlborough in the east to Avebury in the west. But there is no traffic. Everything has stopped. A man in a dark green RAF flight suit runs up and squats down by Kadian. I don't know where he has come from. Could an ambulance have arrived already? Who would have called them? My brain cannot make sense of this collapsed world. 'Is it OK if I turn him over?' he asks. How am I meant to know? I realise it won't make a difference, but the man's question makes me wonder, is there hope? I nod. Cradling his head, he gently pulls one side of Kadian's body over so that he is staring at the sky. He takes out a phone. He's talking to the emergency services.

These images flick through my brain. I notice that I am not holding him. I notice that I am not trying to resuscitate him. I notice that I know there's no point. My brain is observing, detached, helplessly trying to catch up.

At some point I remove his black bicycle helmet, thinking that the strap may reduce the airflow to his brain. I am not sure when I do this. Is it before the man in the green flight suit arrives, or after? Is it before Kadian is turned over? I think it probably is, but I am not sure. Time has ended. There is only this moment, this spot.

My sister arrives. She squats down and holds my head, tight.

'He's dead,' I say to her. 'He's dead.'

'We don't know that yet,' she says. 'Don't give up hope.'

I think for the first time about my wife, Debora, of having to tell her. I start wailing again. No, no, no.

It's been about two minutes since the accident.

Yet, curiously, part of my brain still has hope. I call my uncle – he is a doctor, he might be able to help. My aunt picks up the phone. I tell her what has happened. She does not understand that it is Kadian. But the panic in my voice registers, and she scrambles to find my uncle.

*

'I need to call Deb,' I say to my sister.

'Wait,' she says. 'Let's see what happens.'

'No. I need to call her now. She needs to know.'

It's as though I am standing at the edge of a well. I am out of my mind, all is quiet, nothing is moving. I lean towards the deep hole.

Something clicks in my head, and I realise that I have to make sure there is someone with Deb when I tell her what has happened. Deb is away in America. She is the CEO of a bicycle business. I call her office in Washington DC.

I ask to be put through to the general manager, Gin.

'Hi, Gin. Where's Deb?'

'She's gone out. To the post office, I think,' says Gin. She is calm.

'Gin, Kadian has been in a very bad accident. I need you to be there when I tell Deb. Can you find her? I'll call you back in a few minutes.'

She agrees, and says she will have Nate there as well, the young guy who runs the head office.

A few minutes later I call again. I am put through.

'What's going on?' It's Deb. I know this voice. It is fear. Everything in my body is screaming not to tell her. 'What's happened?'

I'm over the edge now, about to lose my balance. How can I do this to her? I quickly review the options again: Can I delay telling her? Am I being premature? What would I want in this situation? I know what I must do.

'It's Kadian.'

'What do you mean, "it's Kadian"?'

'He's been in an accident.'

'What kind of accident?

'His bike.'

'Well, how bad is it? Has he broken an arm? Did he go over the handlebars?'

'It's bad, Deb. It's bad.'

I can't tell her.

'Well, how bad is bad?'

'Deb,' I say.

'Is he dead?' she asks, her voice louder. I can hear that she is crying.

'Deb,' I say again.

'Is he dead?'

'I don't know,' I finally say. 'It's bad, Deb, it's bad.'

'Where are you?' she asks.

'We're at the roadside, waiting for an ambulance.'

'Who are you with?' She is trying to fill in the details.

'I'm with Amanda and Taylor.'

'Is Sam with you?'

'No.'

And then the phone cuts out. I have lost reception.

Sam. Our daughter Sam. Where is she? I have no idea. Perhaps she is with my parents. How am I going to tell her?

I hand the phone to my sister who tries to call Deb back. I tell her that we need to find someone to be with her. A close friend. Someone who can bring her home. And then I realise how long it will be till she arrives. It is just past six in the evening; even if she catches the next flight she won't be here until six or seven the next morning. I can't believe she isn't with us now. I can't believe that she has to wait, that I can't comfort her.

*

I am now sitting on the kerb. Kadian is still lying on the black tarmac, thirty feet away. The ambulance arrives. Three men walk towards him, very slowly. They lift him into the ambulance and close the doors. There is a finality about this. He is there. I am here.

A policeman walks up to me and introduces himself. He tells me his name, PC James Trafford. He looks young, nervous, unsure. 'I am so sorry,' he enunciates, slowly, as though speaking to a foreigner. 'I won't trouble you now, but at some point, I will need to gather some details.' My sister steps up and says that she can provide all the information he needs. The two of them walk a few steps away, Trafford taking notes in a small black book.

A bright orange medevac helicopter arrives. It lands on the A4, its rotors beating the air. The helicopter paramedics walk to the ambulance. Soon after this my uncle arrives. I ask him to find out what's going on. He steps away and returns a few minutes later and says that they are doing all they can.

I look up to my right and for the first time I see the white van parked a hundred feet up the road. Between the van and the kerb sits a young man, with short curly hair, perhaps in his twenties. He is by himself, staring at the ground.

'Is that the driver?' I ask my nephew.

'I think so,' he says.

I stand up and walk towards him. My nephew tries to stop me, but I tell him it's OK. PC Trafford now hurries after me, but I get to the driver first.

The driver turns as I approach and stands up. I put out my hand; I am not sure if he will take it. He does.

'I am the father,' I say, oddly calm, in control. 'I just want you to know it was not your fault.' The driver looks at me, doesn't move. I turn and leave before he has a chance to respond. I have said what I needed to say.

Kadian is still in the ambulance with the doctors. I close my eyes and speak to him. If you can hear me, Kads, I say, come back. I know you can do it. Come back. I repeat this mantra in my head a hundred times. Come back, Kads, you can do it, come back.

I am gripped by a strong urge to talk to him. I am compelled. It is more than a sense that I have nothing to lose. I feel a vibrant connection with him.

I pace up and down the road; from the ambulance, to the van, then back to the ambulance again, an oval of prayer. At some point I see Kadian's helmet, at the side of the road. Did I put it there? I pick it up and clutch it as I walk back and forth. Nobody interferes with me. I am grateful for the space. It feels sacred. I walk like this alone, waiting, empty.

*

I had never wanted a child. I just didn't see myself as a father. My life was too busy. There was too much that needed to be done.

It was the spring of 1997, and Deb and I were living in Oxford, where we helped run a radical video production company called Undercurrents. Reporting 'the news you don't see on the news', we supported an army of video activists who recorded protests up and down the country: environmentalists who lived in trees hoping to stop a road being built; a group of women who were sent to prison for hammering on an aeroplane carrying nuclear warheads; animal rights campaigners breaking into laboratories; grandmothers who complained about obnoxious fumes emitted by a nearby aluminium factory.

I was away from home a great deal, filming my own stories or running video training workshops. I stayed up late editing. Our house was always full of colourful characters. Our incomes were well below the poverty line. I had been arrested for filming protests in England, the USA, Brazil and Spain. I was too busy to be a father. Too irresponsible.

By this stage we had been married for five years and we were tired of being asked when were going to have kids. Sometimes we told people that we had established a group called Couples Against Kids.

One day I met my cousin James for lunch, and the conversation turned to parenthood. I patiently listed all the reasons why I didn't want to have children, and he smiled understandingly, and asked, 'So, what would you say if Deb told you she was pregnant?'

I paused. 'That would be fantastic!'

'Well, there you go.'

A month later Deb told me it was time. I pride myself on being rational, logical, yet there was no question in my mind that she had formed a connection to this thing, this presence.

There is a video of us from this time. Deb is dressed in an olive-coloured jumpsuit, sitting in a grey-and-purple paisley wing-backed chair that we had picked up from a dump. Giggling with anticipation, she tells me, the cameraman, that she is about to take a pregnancy test. She talks in a baby voice – sweet, innocent, full of light.

She then grabs the camera and points it at me. 'Go on,' she encourages, 'talk, it will be so great if we can all watch this in the future.'

Feigning coyness, I resist, for a while, as though I'm embarrassed to meet my future child. But I relent, of course. Pulling a sheet of paper from my pocket I read a poem that I'd written earlier that day about the pregnancy test. The camera wobbles, and I speak, slowly, nervously: 'This is my big test / can I be who I need to be . . . it seems like the biggest decision of my life / and yet the decision has already been taken.'

'OK,' Deb says when I've finished. 'Let's do it.'

I take the camera again and follow her towards the bathroom. The camera shakes, the pine floor sweeps across the viewfinder, a flush can be heard, and then a white plastic stick is held in front of the camera. There is one line.

'It takes a minute,' Deb says, off-camera.

Still nothing. Perhaps it was all going to be a great disappointment. Then something appears, a faint blue line, and now it's stronger. Deb shrieks with joy and the camera looks around, she is not there, then she is, dancing up and down. 'We're going to have a baby!' she shouts. 'We're going to have a baby!'

I join in the ecstatic chant, 'We're going to have a baby!'

*

He is wearing a bright orange jumpsuit made of a thick fabric – perhaps it is waterproof – with reflective stripes on the shoulders, reinforced padding on the elbows and knees, and a walkie-talkie attached to his chest.

His face is thick with perspiration. Beads of sweat drip from his nose and chin. He crouches down next to me. What would cause a man to sweat like this? I wonder to myself. Could resuscitation be this exhausting? It is warm outside, but not that warm. It couldn't be much hotter in the ambulance.

I know what this is. I have seen it enough times on TV.

'He's dead, isn't he?' I ask.

'We did all that we could,' says the man in the orange suit. 'For an hour we tried to bring him back. I'm very sorry to say . . .' he pauses, 'that we were not successful.'

So that is it. I have just been told that my son is dead. My fourteen-year-old son. Kadian. I had known it from the first moment, but some small part of me had retained hope. All I can do is shake my head. Left and right. Left and right.

I must speak to Deb. Ever since I had first spoken to her she has been on the phone, trying to stay calm, holding on to hope. She has heard the helicopter arriving. She was given regular updates on Kadian's condition. She has discussed which hospital Kadian would be taken to. She still hopes that he will survive.

After a few attempts I am able to get through to her.

'It's me,' I say. 'I've just spoken to one of the medical people.' I stop, for just a few more seconds, and then I say it. 'He's dead, Deb. They've declared he's dead.'

And then she screams. And screams. I keep the phone to my ear. This is real. This is happening. I am numb.

Then a voice.

'Hi, Thomas, it's Nate. What shall I do?'

I can still hear the screaming, a long continuous guttural scream of pain, but it is distant now. Perhaps Nate has walked to another room.

'Nate, you're going to have to figure it out.' And I hand the phone to someone, I cannot remember who, I want to keep the line open.

The helicopter leaves. It is no longer needed.

Now I am falling. And I know the falling won't stop. I am

plummeting head first, down the shaft of a bottomless black well.

Waves of madness shoot through my body. This is beyond pain. I'm sobbing uncontrollably.

I am now in a very deep, dark place, like the inside of a theatre, without light, without chairs, small and alone. The only thing I can hear is a buzzing sound in my ears. I let go. Someone, my nephew maybe, is holding me. I have never been held this tight before. This is more than a hug. This is being clasped to sanity, to humanity.

My uncle crouches down next to me. Touches me on the arm.

'Do you want to see Kadian?' he asks.

I don't. Why would I want to? I have seen him on the ground. The idea of seeing him inside the cramped ambulance – with its gurney and stethoscope and syringes and sterile light – fills me with terror.

'I don't think so,' I say.

'Sometimes people in these situations find it helpful,' he says.

People in these situations. My mind tries to make sense of this sentence. There are 'situations' like this. How can that be possible? How can there be more of this?

I am unsure, but I trust my uncle, he is a good doctor, and I love him. I walk towards the ambulance, wondering if there will be anyone inside. Wanting there to be, not wanting there to be. The doors are closed, I twist the handle and step into the vehicle.

He is alone, a cream-coloured blanket covering his body. His head absolutely still. His face is paler than it should be. His body unmoving. My boy, who had only moments before been full of life and beauty, humour and kindness, is lying dead on this bed.

I cannot touch him. I cannot look at him. I turn and push my way out of the ambulance, and stumble into the open.

*

The birth was a bit of a disaster.

Our house in Oxford was tiny. It was a two-bedroom Victorian terrace, with a spiral staircase twisting up from the ground floor, but we'd made it our own. We had a 'womb room', painted scarlet red, with matching scarlet velvet curtains, a scarlet armchair and sofa, along with a black hairdryer that had been turned into a standing light. There was a 'black room', where Deb had coated the walls with black enamel – we wouldn't be thanked by the next buyers – with a life-sized painting of the goddess Artemis on one wall, and a series of jumping dolphins on another.

As soon as we knew we were pregnant – and it was always 'we' who were pregnant, much to the amusement of my family and friends – we knew that we wanted the birth to be as natural as possible. 'I want to feel the whole thing,' Deb told me bravely, 'I don't want to be off my head on drugs when my baby comes into the world.'

We tackled the birth as we would any new experience – we bought lots of books, and were supremely confident that all would go according to plan. Our doctor had even told us that Deb would be 'up and about' within a few hours of the birth.

It was around eleven o'clock at night on 28 January 1998 when Deb's waters broke. She was asleep at the time. We were staying at my parents' house in London. After a quick goodbye, we climbed into our car and drove the hour and a half back to Oxford.

At three o'clock in the morning, about four hours into labour, Deb decided to take a hot bath in our sauna-like, pine-clad bathroom. I helped light some candles around the bath's edge and then, thinking that I'd need a good place to sit, I attempted to bring our large wing-backed armchair up the spiral staircase. But it wouldn't fit. So, in my state of high anxiety, I began unscrewing all the bolts holding the rail in place, hoping that this would provide enough space to squeeze the chair through. Half an hour later, the rail was hanging limply to one side – we never were able to bolt it back correctly – and the chair would still not fit, so I gave up trying. Instead, I tried to carry a large lamp upstairs, to make sure we had plenty of light during the birth. On the way up I stumbled, bumped my head and dropped the lamp which shattered on the stairs. 'Ahhh!' I shouted. 'I'm bleeding!'

Deb called out in concern from the bathroom, a contraction hitting her at the same time. I told her it was fine, nothing to worry about. She said she thought it might be time to get out of the bath. Leaving the glass on the stairs I went into the bathroom and grabbed a towel to help her out. But I'd forgotten about the candles around the bath edge and, as I went to wrap the towel around my pregnant wife's body, she screamed. 'It's on fire! The towel's on fire!'

After that, we decided that it might be better if I waited downstairs until the midwife came.

The labour itself was hard, and long. After fourteen hours we gave up on our home-delivery plan and were happy to be transferred to the Radcliffe Infirmary, our local hospital.

We were quickly admitted and moved into a birthing room. Deb was exhausted and in agony, and asking for pain relief. The doctor refused. He said that it was too late for an epidural. I knew that there were other choices, such as nitrous oxide, which he wasn't offering. I felt a wave of tremendous anger surge through my body. I hated this man. For hurting my wife, for putting my child in jeopardy. I wanted to punch him in the face.

I had never had this feeling before, blind rage, raw aggression towards another person. I knew it would be counterproductive to take a swing at him, I wasn't even sure I would connect as I had never hit anyone before in my life, but the urge gripped me. Later, when I was at home and I told a friend about my feelings, she said that I looked different somehow, not just because I was a father, but because I was a father who was compelled to protect his wife and child.

When at last Kadian was pulled out – with a device that looked like a toilet plunger, and I do seem to remember there was actually a popping noise – his head was huge (ninety-seven percentile for skull size), purple and cone-shaped. I was shocked, a little grossed out, but totally in love.

The nurse took him to one side, carried out a few basic tests, and handed him back to Deb. I have never seen my wife so happy. She glowed with love. She was a mother. I was a father. We had a beautiful baby boy.

*

Why did this happen?

We had been cycling down the hill, laughing, calling out to each other, a family out on a bike ride, a day to remember. There had been no threat, no sign of danger, no cause for concern.

How was this possible? Kadian was an experienced cyclist. Nobody else had difficulty stopping in time. He must have seen the road ahead, he was at least three hundred feet away from the intersection when he had first emerged from the trees. Why hadn't he stopped?

Was it the brakes? We had been worried that they hadn't been working properly, but Kadian had gone to a bike shop to have them fixed that day. They couldn't have failed.

My brain snaps into a new mode. I am aware of a visceral shift in my mental function, from one part of my brain to another, almost as if it was from one brain to another.

Walking over to the front of the van I notice that Kadian's bike is stuck in its front grille, suspended vertically. Somehow the handlebars had become enmeshed and the bike had been carried forward. The windscreen is smashed, a circle of crushed glass radiating from the left-hand side. This must have been where he had been hit. Thrown up onto the windscreen as the van struck the bike, then tossed to the side, all at great speed. The van had been moving so fast. Had he died instantly? Or was it when he hit the road? Did he know what was happening? Did he have time to feel fear? A new wave of terror pulses through my body.

*

We didn't know what to call him. Deb had always believed it would be a boy, from the moment we'd conceived. And when it was confirmed at our first scan, we realised we had to find a name. Throughout the pregnancy we had referred to him as

'Stodge'. We purchased a couple of name books and for a few days mulled over Christopher, Bartholomew, Wilbur, but nothing fitted.

Then one day, Deb met a woman on a train as she was travelling to Brighton. The woman had spotted Deb's bump – by this time Deb was enormous, beyond any stage where someone might tentatively ask – and they got to talking about names. The woman said that she had only daughters, but had been saving a special name for a boy. 'Kadian,' she said. 'It's Jamaican. It means cheerful and charming.'

And from the very start, he was.

He smiled at his mother when the nurse first handed him over. He smiled on the changing mat. He smiled at the doctors, even as he was put on a cold metal weighing scale.

As the weeks progressed, his cheeriness only intensified. Gurgling happily in a blue sling as we walked down the street. Chortling as he slithered his way for the first time across the living room's hardwood floor. Laughing as he spooned his own mashed bananas into his mouth, dropping most of the goop onto his Tigger-patterned onesie. He was great company as a baby. His equanimity and joy of life was a gift.

I had decided early on, before Kadian was born, that I would be an equal parent. I took this quite seriously.

Few of my male friends had children and those that did played at best a minor role in the childcare department. Typically they took a couple of weeks off around the birth and tried, when they could, to be home for bathtime. The women, the vast majority of whom had jobs, were expected to take on the lion's share. This didn't seem right to me. I wanted something different. I wanted to be an equal parent.

Maybe it was the fact that my father had been absent when I

was a child. Maybe it was the feminism course I'd taken at university. Maybe it was because I was curious to see what this new universe would be like. Most likely it was a combination of all of the above.

It quickly became part of my identity, part of my story. I was the man who chose to take care of his child, not because of our careers, but because I wanted to be involved, day-to-day, with my perfect newborn son.

It didn't start too well. When Kadian was only three weeks old I was changing him on our changing table: a pine chest of drawers topped with a blue plastic mat that I had inherited from my older brother. I pulled off his soiled cloth nappy, threw it into a basket – they were picked up by a reusable nappy service, who cleaned, boiled and returned the nappies, neatly folded – and wiped him down. I left Kadian on the mat, and walked a few paces to the bathroom to look for the baby powder. A few seconds later I heard a thud. There was no cry. I hurried back and found Kadian on the floor. He had, somehow, rolled twelve inches to the edge of the mat, and fallen three feet to the hard pine floor below.

I picked him up. His eyes were closed; he made no sound; most worryingly he didn't seem to be breathing. With him in my arms, I rushed to the phone and called 999, begging the operator to send an ambulance as quickly as possible. By the time we reached the hospital at least fifteen minutes had elapsed, and just as we walked through the doors he opened his eyes and started breathing normally again. He appeared to react well to all the tests, and the doctors assured me that he had only knocked himself unconscious for a brief period. He would probably be fine. Probably.

From this point on I was terrified of Kadian getting hurt, and fully aware that I, as the father, as the caretaker, was the person who had to protect him.

*

I look again at the bicycle. He was so proud of this bike. Only a few days before we had filmed Kadian joyfully withdrawing it, item by item, from a large plastic container. Now its back wheel is crumpled, its brake pads hang below the rim. The front brakes look as if they have not been damaged, the cables appear to be in place. What had really happened on that slope? Am I allowed to take photographs? I don't care. I remove my phone from my pocket. A grieving father turned crime-scene investigator.

Had there really not be enough time to stop? I stride back down the road, past the van and the ambulance, back towards the hill we had been riding down. PC Trafford approaches. He tells me I can't go up, I may disturb the evidence. 'It's important that we find out what happened,' he says gently. 'The forensic team will want to examine the bicycle tracks.'

'I'll be careful,' I say, walking up the hill, not giving him a choice.

I follow the edge of the track where the grass still grows, avoiding the central gravelly area where we had freewheeled just an hour before. At the top of the slope, just before the woods start, I turn round. I can clearly see the A4 in the distance – three hundred feet away. More than enough distance for an experienced cyclist like Kadian to have stopped. How the hell had this happened? Could the bike shop have messed up the repair? Is it possible that my son was now dead because some idiot didn't pay attention?

Somewhere, deep inside, I feel the first rumblings of caustic anger – sharp, searing I-am going-to-murder-someone anger.

*

You could say that Kadian had been born from a bike. Debora and I met when we took part in Bike Aid, a coast-to-coast charity ride across America in 1987. Our route would take nine weeks, and snaked over three thousand miles across the US, from Portland, Oregon, on the west coast to Washington DC on the east.

There were thirty of us in all, mostly students. We slept in high school gyms and church halls. Along the way we took part in community projects, painting an elderly couple's home in Dayton, Ohio, and helping disadvantaged kids in Chicago fix their bikes. In Jackson Hole, Wyoming, we served pancakes during the Fourth of July parade. In South Dakota we were inducted into the Sioux tribe. In Manhattan, the traffic was halted as the police escorted us down Fifth Avenue to the United Nations building.

The ride was a wonderful way to experience America: the waterfalls dumping off the Oregonian Cascades, the craggy tips of the Grand Tetons, the endless fields of maize in Nebraska. By travelling at a slower pace than a car or bus, and by stopping often, it also gave us an opportunity to meet people, the everyday folk who inhabited middle America.

Cycling across country was also a wonderful way to fall in love. Debora was five years older than me, a political activist who had spent years working for the senator and Democratic presidential candidate Gary Hart. She was smart, funny, feisty and extremely beautiful. It was every English schoolboy's dream: a summer spent with a hot American girl.

*

I am desperate to talk to Deb, but I can't get a connection for very long. It is during one of these brief conversations that we discuss how we should break the news to Sam. What will I say?

'I want you to wait till I'm there,' says Deb. 'As a mother I need to be there when she hears the news.'

I understand. I would want the same. To be able to share this shocking, awful news, to be able to hold her, reassure her, answer her questions, to be together. But I know that we cannot wait. Like Deb, Sam has to be told immediately.

I suggest that Deb should be on the phone when I speak to Sam. Deb agrees.

A few minutes later my uncle Michael returns. He is with his wife, my aunt Angela. I have never seen her lost for words before. She may have mouthed 'I'm so sorry'. She may have said nothing. What I do remember is that she gave me a strong hug – solid, firm, grounded, tethered to the earth. This is more of a physical memory than a visual one, as if this hug has been printed on my body. I can still feel it.

*

Fourteen months after Kadian was born, his sister, Sam, arrived. Her delivery was much easier.

This time we had a tub, the size of a small paddling pool, set up in our kitchen. Deb's sister was on hand, as was our good friend Cait. There was no laughing gas or last-minute trips to the hospital. After three hours of labour, Sam simply swam out of her mother, who was lying against me in the pool.

Unlike her brother, Sam was quiet and cautious. She didn't like anyone but us holding her. If anyone approached she would flash them a stern look. While Kadian happily slept with us in our bed for nine months, Sam needed her own space.

Kadian celebrated his first birthday only a few weeks before Sam was born. He took his first step the day after she was born. As such, he was too young to register what life was like without a sister.

They were attached from the very beginning. Kadian showed Sam the world. She would mimic his behaviour and then check to see if she had done it correctly. She would watch him eat. They sat on the potty next to each other. They picked flowers together. He pushed her around in a small wooden cart. They had baths together. They went to nursery together, sitting side by side in a yellow-and-blue bicycle buggy. It wasn't till she was three and a half years old that we realised she hadn't really started talking yet. Kadian did all the talking for her.

Sam grew at a fast rate and brother and sister soon appeared to be the same age. We joked that they were 'Irish Twins'. When I was away and spoke to them by phone I could not tell their voices apart. They had the same blond hair, the same nose, the same freckle on the inside of their right hand's fourth finger, the same cute accent, English mixed with a little American.

They were inseparable.

*

I climb into the passenger seat of my uncle's car. I am about to leave the place where my son has been killed. Time, that has stopped, will start again. There will be a new geography, a new landscape that I will have to navigate. I find this awkward, impossible to process. As we drive off, my brain fogs, my body feels disconnected from the leather seat I am sitting in, the fabric of the belt tight across my chest. I feel like I am in a flight simulator, the images of the road and cars and buildings flashing in front of me, virtual and unimportant. A chasm is developing between my senses and my reality.

'There are a lot of people at the house,' my aunt says from the back seat. 'Do you want them there or would you like them to leave so that you can be alone with Sam?'

'Alone, please,' I say. She places a call, and speaks quietly into the phone.

A few minutes later we arrive at my parents' house, a pretty red-brick building with a thatched roof that stands by itself at the edge of a village on the eastern side of Marlborough. Thankful that there is no line of family members waiting to greet me at the gate, I walk through the living room to the glass-sided summer room, where I have been told Sam is waiting. I can see in her eyes that she knows there is something wrong.

'What's happened?' she asks. 'Nobody's told me anything.'

'Something horrible has happened. Kadian has had an accident,' I say slowly. I am standing in front of her. Not touching her, but very close. I know what this is going to do. 'Sam, it's terrible. He was on his bike, he was hit by a van, he is dead.'

She howls. Like her mother. And collapses on the ground. Why? Why? Why? I am holding her now. She physically fights the terror, trying to push it away with her hands. My aunt walks over to me, crouches down and embraces us both. I am detached. Watching the scene from a distance. Glad that I am not alone. After a few moments I tell Sam that her mother is on the phone – I do not remember calling, perhaps someone else did – and wants to talk to her. I pass the phone and Sam is listening; I can't hear the words but I can tell they are soothing, for Sam calms a little. 'I love you too,' says Sam to her mother, 'I love you so much.' I take the phone and pass it to someone – again, I'm not sure who. I focus on my daughter. She has no brother now, I think to myself. She will be alone. No one to talk to. No one to complain about us to. It will be so quiet in the house. Just the three of us. How will it feel when she turns fifteen, and she will become older than her brother? Is thirteen too young to remember your brother? All these thoughts fire through my brain like cattle stampeding through a tunnel.

'Promise me,' says Sam, through her tears. 'Pinkie-promise that you won't feel guilty,' she says. A pinkie-promise cannot be broken.

I clasp her pinkie with mine. 'I promise,' I say.

'And promise me,' I say, 'that we will live every day to the full, for Kadian.'

And as I do, I wonder if this is possible.

*

As toddlers, Kadian and Sam were music lovers. They were always begging us to 'play the tape', in the car on the way to the supermarket or on the stereo in the living room.

They had their favourites, of course, such as 'The Wheels on the Bus Go Round and Round' and 'Puff, the Magic Dragon'. They knew exactly where these songs started on the tape cassette and would insist that we played them over and over again.

But there was one tune that united the family and, no matter our moods or where we were located, once we heard the first few bars, we ran to the kitchen and began dancing around the table. It was 'All Around the Kitchen Cock-a-doodle-doo', and with the music blaring, we jived and jigged as the song instructed us: 'Stop right there . . . put your hands in the air . . . Put your hands on your hip . . . turn all around . . . and you do a silly dance' and on and on.

Finally, the track would stop, leaving us all laughing and gasping for breath, exhilarated by such unrepressed silliness. Then, having recovered, we would return to whatever activity had been interrupted.

*

Various family members start to appear in the room. Aunts, uncles, cousins, my brother, my sisters, my parents. Within two hours there are over forty people in the house. It is not a large building, yet I am left, for the most part, to myself.

At some stage PC Trafford enters along with a community liaison officer. I instantly dislike her. She seems too eager to please, too artificial, talking to us as if reading from a script. I excuse myself and walk upstairs.

How long has it been since we arrived at the house? The hours spin by unnoticed. My cousin James joins us. He is like a brother to me. We are similar in age and have been through a lot together. He knows me and loves me and has wisdom in spades. He has watched Kadian and Sam grow up, he is a part of their lives. Together with Sam, we go outside.

It is pitch black now. Besides a slight pinkish glow from Swindon to the north, there is little light pollution in this valley. On the wet grass we drop long green-and-blue striped cushions and lie down under the stars, our bodies touching, to keep warm.

'I wonder if he's up there,' I say.

'Where would he be?' James asks.

'There, at the end of the Big Dipper,' says Sam, pointing. 'The bright twinkly one.'

The three of us look at the star. I can't believe that I am lying here talking about which star Kadian is. My heart is racing too fast for my immobile state of being, my eyes pool with tears. We remain outside for an hour or so, increasingly chilled but glad to be on our own.

I tell Sam that I think we should sleep next to each other. We go inside and get under the blankets. I hold Sam tight. 'I can't believe this happening,' she says. 'Me neither,' I say. 'Me neither.'

*

In 1999, we moved to Charlbury, a charming little village just outside Oxford. The houses in the village were built of yellow limestone. The Evenlode, a narrow, grass-banked river flowed next to a twelfth-century church. There was a station from which trains ran directly to Oxford, and then on to London, a post office which doubled up as a grocer's, an estate agent's, an independent bookshop, a nursery, two playgrounds and two old pubs with low ceilings, each boasting large inglenook fireplaces, both serving locally brewed beer. It seemed like an idyllic place to bring up two small children.

Our new home sat at the bottom of an old quarry, a lush bowl carved into the earth. It was called 'Bag End'. According to the previous owner, J. R. R. Tolkien had granted him permission to use the name back in the 1950s after he put on the first theatrical performance of *The Hobbit*.

The house hadn't been updated since the 1960s. The floors were covered with mouldy pink carpets, the painted wooden trim was peeling, the few windows it had offered scant light, rendering the house dark and foreboding. The front door was so low that even I had to bend to enter.

We set about transforming it into our dream family house. We demolished the internal walls on the ground floor, forming a massive open kitchen. We knocked through new windows, widened the existing ones and added skylights to a few ceilings.

We pulled up all the carpets and replaced them with stone and hardwood floors.

And we began to landscape the gardens. One day Kadian came home from nursery to find a giant yellow machine in the garden. 'It's a bulldozer!' he shouted. For months he had been a fan of the television programme *Bob the Builder*. Every night, after their baths, Kadian and Sam would bounce on our bed singing at the top of their voices: 'Bob the Builder, can he fix it? Bob the Builder, YES HE CAN!'

'Can we drive it?' Kadian asked. I hoisted him up to the cab and climbed in after. I then lifted him onto my lap and watched with pleasure as he pulled levers and pushed buttons, all the while singing, 'Bob the Builder, can he fix it? Bob the Builder, YES HE CAN!'

*

The alarm on my iPhone goes off. It is 5.45 in the morning. Deb is arriving on the seven o'clock flight from Washington DC. It will take an hour for us to drive to the airport, I want to make sure we arrive before she does. James says he will be outside at six to collect us. I am anxious and edgy.

At two minutes past six I pull out my phone to find out where he is. Before I can press 'call' we see his car coming down the road towards us. Sam and I climb in. James's mother, my aunt, has thoughtfully packed us a bag of food and drink. A blanket is lying across the back seat. There are people who are taking care of us. Who act with confidence and sureness. It makes me feel a little less unstable, a little less unmoored.

How will Deb be?

She has flown over with Dominic, our very close friend. He had been at home in Shepherdstown, West Virginia, when he received a phone call from Deb. It was about an hour after she had learned that Kadian had died. Kadian had grown up in Shepherdstown, and had spent much time with Dom and his three daughters. We had coached football together, canoed down rivers together, shared numerous barbecues together. When Dom had received her call he had said he would be at the airport within the hour. I will forever be grateful to him for this. The idea of Deb flying alone fills me with dread.

I sit in the middle of a row of moulded black plastic chairs, James's hand resting gently on my knee. Sam sits next to me. We wait.

My descent down the dark well has been momentarily halted, as if I have landed on a ledge. Though minutes flow past, time remains still, stuck in the accident's frame.

Then the large double doors swing open and there is Deb, with Dom. Our eyes meet, her lips wobble, all strength that I have flows out of my legs, I can't move. Her being here makes it real. She is still on the other side of the arrivals barrier, then we are holding each other. 'I can't believe it,' she is saying. 'I'm so glad you're here,' I say. 'What are we going to do?' she asks. 'What are we going to do?' I say. 'Is he really gone?' she asks. 'I can't believe it,' I say.

Two policemen stand close by. I hadn't noticed them until now. Apparently they had escorted Deb and Dom from the plane, sped them through passport control, trying to make it as easy as was possible given the circumstances. 'Given the circumstances', a phrase which was to be repeated often over the next few months and is one of my least favourite English expressions, for it is so vague yet hints at indescribable horror.

Dom gives me a hug. 'I'm so sorry, brother,' he says. Tears

are in his eyes. I thank him for being with Deb. He tells me that she was amazing on the flight. Talked most of the way, recalling Kadian stories, special times together. She didn't sleep more than a few minutes.

'We'll accompany you out of the airport,' the tall policeman says, after a few moments. We walk, a posse of grief, to James's car. Deb is holding Sam tight, though it is clear that our daughter is the sturdier of the pair.

In the car Sam sits between me and Deb. We are all in shock; this is foreign territory. I am aware of being detached, my senses disconnected from my mental functions. The police escort us to a petrol station just outside the airport. My cousin steps out and thanks them for their support. And then we are on our way back to my parents' house. We don't talk for a long time, we just hold each other, close.

Then, in a quiet voice, Deb asks me to describe what happened. When it comes to the moment when Kadian is hit by the van, I am crying so much I can barely speak. Sam puts her arm around me, I tuck my head into the gap between her neck and shoulder. We sit there like this for a while, in silence.

Then Deb says, 'So he died instantly? He didn't feel anything? He didn't know?'

'I don't think so,' I say. 'I knew he was dead as soon as I saw him. His eyes, they didn't move. His pupils were fixed, they were so large.'

Deb hasn't stopped crying. 'Thank God,' she says, 'thank God that he didn't feel any pain. And thank God that you were there at the end.'

There is a pause, and then Deb turns to me: 'Did you have him take the bike in to have the brakes fixed?'

I feel the question like a hammer blow to the head.

'Yes,' I say. 'I gave him money, and told him to take it to a bike shop in town. He went a few hours before the accident. To the shop next to Waitrose, in Marlborough. He told me they'd fixed the brakes.'

'I'm so relieved,' she says, crying. 'On the flight here I kept thinking that I didn't know what I was going to do if you hadn't.'

The dam, at least for now, holds steady.

Deep inside the fog that is my current mental state I register that we have narrowly avoided a second calamity. I fleetingly wonder what it would feel like to go through this without my wife, with my daughter torn between us. Somehow I know that this won't happen now. I am thankful, but I feel no relief.

There is another long silence as we make our way back to Wiltshire. From the front seat, James observes how moved he is, listening to us, the way in which each of us takes care of the other in turn, Sam to me, me to Deb, Deb to me, me to Sam and so on. I hear his words, I know they are formed by love, I sense the outline of their meaning, but I can't feel the warmth contained within.

The blue-and-white signs of the M4 flick past: Slough, Reading, Newbury, Hungerford, Marlborough.

*

We befriended an eccentric lady who lived near our house in Charlbury. Mad Mabel we called her. She was a small woman, perhaps in her sixties, who dressed like a gypsy fortune-teller and ran an animal sanctuary.

Soon we had two pot-bellied pigs (Bilbo and Baggins), two albino rabbits (Jelly and Jam), two peacocks (Romeo and Juliet), two cats (their names now forgotten), and a Border collie (Molly), with one green eye and one blue eye, who kept running away.

On the way to nursery Kadian would help me feed the pigs, and when he returned home later in the afternoon, he would visit them again and ask me how they had spent their day.

While Sam took her afternoon nap, we found ways to fill the time. With Kadian standing on a chair so he could reach the table, and with an apron tied round his little waist, we made loaves of banana bread and trays of chocolate-chip cookies. I read to him stories of Christopher Robin and his friend Winnie-the-Pooh. We studied the letters of the alphabet and counted backwards from twenty. We draped sheets between our sofas and imagined that we were knights in a castle with a dragon for a pet. We told each other jokes with made-up words.

When the weather was nice, we snuck into the abandoned quarry behind our house. Kadian skipped along the path, I carried Sam on my back. Once inside the quarry, we searched for sparkly crystals in the rock face. On the way home, we stopped at the playground in the large field next to our house. While I held Sam or gave her a bottle, Kadian climbed the brightly coloured apparatus. 'Look at me, Dad,' he would shout as he slid down a short slide, before clambering back up. 'Look at me.'

From our village we took the 'choo choo' train into Oxford. In the winter we visited the stuffed dodo in the big museum, in the summer we brought a picnic and punted along the river.

It was a wonderful place to be a small person. To be active. To be alive.

*

Deb says she wants to go and see Kadian as soon as possible. I tell her that he is in Swindon hospital, we will have to call to set up an appointment. James asks how we want things at home. I hadn't thought about this. I don't think I can deal with everyone back at my parents' house. James calls ahead and gently suggests that everyone has breakfast elsewhere.

Our dear friends Jane and Greg arrive a few minutes after us. They have five children of their own, and their eldest, Edy, was born six days prior to Kadian. Though we had known each other before, our families were brought together by their two births, and from that time we have shared worlds: birthdays, long Sunday lunches, New Year's Eves, trips abroad. They are wise, they share our values and they have great organisational skills. If anyone has the capacity to help us in this situation, they do.

As soon as I see their faces I appreciate my error. Like us they are crumpled by grief. Strangely, this brings me a sense of comfort. I am not in this by myself. I can share this awful burden. Perhaps that is the way through?

James leaves, and Jane and Greg offer to drive us to the hospital. I tell Deb that I don't want to see Kadian again. I understand why she wants to, and I will go with her to the hospital, but I can't see him. Jane says she will go in with Deb, if she wants her to.

The four of us drive to Swindon General Hospital, an ugly concrete block on the edge of the town. In the hospital's high-ceilinged foyer we meet the police liaison woman again. I still don't like her. There is something about her that repels me. It is as if we are a task. Something to strike off the list. Jane picks up on my distaste and steps in.

The liaison woman invites us to talk in the hospital cafeteria. I say no. How can I discuss my son's body across a sticky hospital table? We ask if there is a private room, but she says there is not. We stand in a small group a few yards from the main entrance, irritated by the small black flies buzzing around our heads, but thankful at least to be in the open air.

The liaison woman asks us a lot of impossible questions. Who will be collecting Kadian's body? And when? Where will he be taken? Who could she talk to about the investigation? Do we have a funeral parlour in mind?

And all the time, I'm thinking about Kadian, lying somewhere downstairs, and wondering, is he cold? Are his eyes still open? How does he look? Will I go in to see him? How will Deb react when she goes in?

We walk downstairs. To the morgue. The morgue, my son in a morgue. My brain cannot process this information. It refuses. I want to leave, to be anywhere but here. We are led into a small waiting area, and sit down in four padded chairs, next to a side table. There is a large box of tissues on the table. It is very quiet in this room.

The liaison woman leaves, and two other women arrive. They are both short, with kindly faces, and dressed in black – black shirts, black trousers. We talk about what happened. They have been here before, they know how this works, yet when Deb says that Kadian was only fourteen, the women's eyes moisten. One of the women has just seen him. 'He is so beautiful,' she says, and apologises.

'Please don't be sorry,' Deb says. 'You should cry, it is very sad.'

Deb stands and asks if she can go and see Kadian now. They say yes, that he is 'ready'. Deb halts a moment, and asks if they have done anything to him, besides clean him up. 'He looks . . . normal,' one of the women says, 'at peace.'

I decide to go in. Greg says that he will come as well. The

door is opened and the four of us walk into a cold, bare beige-coloured room. Kadian is lying on a hospital bed, a thin blanket covering his body, only his face is showing. There is no pillow under his head.

Deb walks up to him, she is crying, love pouring out of her. Stroking his thick brown hair, she speaks quietly to him. She touches his chest, his arm, she pulls back the blanket and looks at his scratched hand. He looks very different from how he did in the ambulance. The horror is gone. He looks peaceful. There is a slight smile on his lips. His eyes are almost closed. His skin is pale and sparkling, as if dusted with light. I don't know why, but today I feel only love and loss.

I look at Deb. There is no fear. She is calm. She continues to stroke Kadian's hair. Jane is crying. Greg stands near the door, panic in his eyes. I am glad that I decided to see Kadian again.

Deb says that she would like to spend time alone with him. The three of us return to the padded seats outside. I desperately want to be as brave as Deb. Instead, I sense my brain busily erecting a wall, behind which I crouch, hiding from the barrage of emotions.

I am a coward.

*

It was the year 2000, and we were now the owners of our own television station. It had all happened quickly. Two years earlier, Deb had heard that the government was going to be handing out licences to anyone wanting to set up a local television station. We had been looking for ways to expand our video production company, to make use of our contacts in the business, to find a job that provided stability, and allowed us to spend more time with the kids. Astonishingly, her application was accepted. Apparently, nobody else applied.

With Deb now holding a licence, I abandoned my career as a radical video maker – much to the chagrin of some of our former colleagues – to help her to set up the station. We moved into a former nuclear bunker for city officials, and grew quickly, employing sixty people, and producing an hour of original television every day. Within a short period, we were watched by 25 per cent of the local population – over 125,000 people.

We only had two problems. The first was childcare. We solved this by sharing the job of managing director, each working part-time and trying to juggle our responsibilities as best we could. But it was hard. I'd often call into meetings while out playing in the park; Deb would breastfeed Sam in her office.

And the second problem was that we were fast running out of money. Despite our best efforts, we were failing to convince local businesses to advertise with us. I was spending more time seeking out potential investors than I was making television programmes.

Eventually we reached a crisis point. In order to save the station, and to protect as many jobs as we could, we sold the company to a local media outfit.

Deb and I were now unemployed, with two small children, two pigs, two cats, two peacocks and a collie who liked to run away. It was more than enough to keep us busy. But after three months we realised that a decision had to be made. One of us was going to have to get a 'real job', which in all likelihood meant taking the train to London every day. It was not an appealing prospect.

Then, one day, we had an idea. What if we could find somewhere else to live, somewhere cheaper than overpriced

Oxfordshire, a place where we could both continue to spend time with Kadian and Sam, and where the kids could grow up outdoors, enjoying and exploring nature?

Six months later we had sold our house and most of our belongings, and were living in a mobile home in a campground in West Virginia.

*

After ten minutes Deb comes out of the room in the hospital basement.

I stand, realising that I also want to say goodbye to Kadian. This surprises me. I walk through the door and I am suddenly alone with my dead son. My first thought is that this is so strange. That he is not moving. That he is no longer alive.

I step to the left of him, put my hand on his arm, and look at his face.

'Hi, Kads,' I say. 'I love you. I love you so much. I can't believe you're not here. Where have you gone?'

I am astonished that I am talking to him, I know that he is dead, that he cannot hear me, that I am speaking to an empty room.

A moment comes back to me from the ride. Just before he headed down the narrow wooded path, Kadian said, 'You are the worst navigator in the world,' in a jokey, teasing tone. I was the worst navigator in the world. I had the map, I had got us lost, I had allowed my fourteen-year-old son to cycle down a path towards a road where cars and vans sped by at sixty miles an hour. What the fuck was I thinking?

'I'm sorry, Kads,' I whisper, crying. 'I'm so sorry, I wish I could have protected you. I failed you as a father.'

I am confused by this confession of guilt. Where has it come from? And I am terrified of where it might lead to. Do I really feel responsible for his death? How am I going to be able to live with that? Is it really my fault?

I lean over and kiss him the way I did each night, when I tucked him in: forehead, chin, left cheek, right cheek, then finally, I wiggle my nose against his. It feels cold. Cold.

I look at him for a few moments longer.

'Bye, Kads,' I say, and then again, 'I love you. Best son in the world.' I wait for him to give his usual reply, 'Best father in the world.' He doesn't, and I walk out.

*

Life in the mobile home, or RV, was a blast, as they say in West Virginia. It was early summer, a great time to be living outdoors. If we wanted to explore, we had pine woods on our doorstep and the Potomac River a short walk away. If we wanted history, we visited the nearby town of Harpers Ferry, where the abolitionist John Brown had led his infamous raid just before the civil war. If we wanted culture, we drove to Washington DC, sixty miles to the south, and spent the afternoon in one of its museums, enjoying the free exhibits and the government-funded air conditioning.

The RV was tiny, with space for only a few items, stored in one of the cupboards above the pullout kitchen table. Our supply of toys, clothes and sundries was severely limited. In many ways this was a blessing, a simple life. It also suited the kids, who made do with what was available.

Best of all was a battery-powered jeep that Taylor, Kadian's cousin, had donated. It was made of brightly coloured yellow plastic and was just about big enough for both Kadian and Sam to sit in. Kadian drove his sister to the campsite's over-chlorinated pool. He drove his sister to the showers. He drove his sister to the shop to buy sweets. Dressed in her blue jean short-shorts and pink spaghetti-strap T-shirt, her sun-bleached hair cut in a bob, sucking a dummy, she would give us a regal wave as her elder brother chauffeured her around the campsite.

The campsite was wonderful in the summer, but we soon began to worry about the winter. Life would be much less fun when everything was covered in snow. After a few weeks of searching we found a detached nineteenth-century house in Shepherdstown, a small college town fifteen miles west of Harpers Ferry.

We moved in only to realise that the property needed to be entirely renovated. We parked the RV in our new garden and returned to our mobile home while we set to work. Walls were taken down. Carpets pulled up. We disconnected and dismantled the old lead pipes which were calcified from a century of use. The whole house was rewired. Its outside was scraped and painted a rich cream, highlighted by deep cobalt blue and burnt orange. We built vegetable boxes in the garden and planted aubergines, courgettes and tomatoes. Deb drew sunsets and dolphins onto the children's bedroom walls.

But we continued to have fun. With some help from Deb and me, Kadian and Sam built a six-foot-high mud man in the garden. Breaking up some old blue and white tiles they had found, they pushed the pieces into the lumpy head to create two startling eyes. They sculpted him a button nose and a wide-lipped mouth, and scattered grass seeds on his bald spot. Pretty soon he was sprouting a handsome head of green hair. It all felt creative, but also a little unstable.

*

From the hospital we drive to the scene of the accident. I am filled with a cocktail of emotions: dread at revisiting the site of my son's death, the site of my failure as a father; anxiety that Deb will find the visit overwhelming, an extreme stimulus in an already highly volatile situation; fear of being trapped back in the nightmare of yesterday; and yearning to be close to Kadian, given that this was the last place that he was alive.

We park on a narrow road just off the A4. I am buffeted by the wind generated by the cars and vans as they whizz by, terrifyingly fast. My body shudders involuntarily, my brain buzzes, I feel light-headed, unsteady, short of breath.

'Where was it?' Deb asks. I point across the road. 'Over there,' I say. There is a piece of plastic lying on the verge. 'That's debris from the accident.'

Once a gap appears in the traffic we run across, past white crosses that have been etched into the asphalt, symbols that this is the site of an accident. Up ahead of us, in front of a small white-brick house, we see PC Trafford talking to a well-built man with dark hair: the man with the flight suit. We walk over.

'This is my wife, Debora,' I say to the two men.

'I am so sorry for your loss,' says PC Trafford, and then introduces the man he's been talking to: 'This is Richard. He witnessed the accident.'

'I just don't understand why he didn't stop,' I blurt out. 'He was an experienced cyclist. The slope isn't that steep. None of the rest of us had any trouble slowing down. Surely the brakes couldn't have failed. He had them checked only a few hours before the ride.'

Richard looks at PC Trafford, waiting for approval to speak. Our son's death has stopped being our story; it is now controlled, at least in a small way, by the state and its officers.

I try again. 'Did you see the accident? It would be very helpful for us to know. I just don't understand what happened.' Richard looks again at PC Trafford. He nods.

'I heard you before I saw you,' Richard starts, 'from the woods, above our house. Shouting and laughing. I could tell you were having a good time. Then I saw your son come down the footpath, he was cycling quite fast, around twenty-five to thirty miles per hour. He wasn't slowing down. He was screaming. I was standing outside my gate just next to the footpath, about fifty feet from the road. By the time he reached me I could tell he was out of control. I thought about jumping in front of him, but there wasn't enough time. I shouted at him to crash into the bushes next to the footpath. I'm not sure if he heard me. I saw him pump the brakes, both brakes, back and front, over and over again, but he wasn't slowing down. Then he entered the road. And he was hit.'

Kadian had been trying to slow down. His brakes had failed. He had been screaming. He had been aware that he was out of control. That he was going to crash. The brakes *had* failed.

Had he seen the van? Did he know he was going to be hit?

Why didn't he jump off the bike? Why had the brakes failed? He had been screaming. And then he had been hit. Oh my God. Poor, poor Kadian.

Stark images flash through my head. The van swiping Kadian from left to right. Me dropping my bike. Kadian face down on the road. The pool of blood by his mouth. My howling.

He had been screaming.

*

I remember teaching Kadian how to ride a bike. He was four.

We were out in the lane behind our new house. He was sitting on his tiny turquoise bike. I had removed his stabilisers. He had a bright blue helmet strapped under his chin. His little gloved hands gripped the handlebars. Black plastic knee guards were pulled up over his brown corduroy trousers. The narrow lane was perfectly smooth and sloped gently downwards between two high hedges. A perfect spot for a beginner.

'Are you ready?' I asked. He gave me a smile and pushed off. He wobbled, straightened up, then gathered speed. 'I'm doing it, I'm doing it!' he cried.

I was now trotting behind him with my hand on his back. I could see the end of the road approaching. He was picking up speed. 'Slow down, Kads, slow down.'

He braked, and quickly came to a halt.

'That was fun!' he said, joy painted across his face. 'Let's do it again!'

I held the bike as he climbed off, and together we walked back up the lane towards the house.

*

We say goodbye to PC Trafford and Richard. Deb wants to go home, to our home, in Hampshire. That feels right to me. I need my own space and quiet to be able to sort things out, for my brain to try and make sense of what is happening to us.

We return to my parents' house to get our things. There are over forty people there. While we are packing, I ask Greg and Dominic to visit the bike shop in Marlborough, to see if the mechanic remembers working on Kadian's bike and, if possible, to collect a receipt for the repairs.

An hour later, they return, just as we are saying goodbye to everyone. The shop owner said that he had worked on Kadian's bike. He remembered working on the brakes, and gave Dominic a receipt confirming it.

We set off for home.

There is a convoy of two cars. My sister Kate has joined us, along with Greg, Jane and James. I am terrified of our house. Kadian's house.

After an hour and a half we arrive in our village, driving past the pub, the village hall, the war memorial. We pull into our gravel driveway. The house is dark, the curtains are pulled tight. I have never seen it look so secure.

We are home.

Now what am I supposed to do?

I sit on the sofa, staring at the fireplace. Behind me I hear someone busy in the kitchen.

Tears slowly roll down my cheeks. I am frozen. I am shaking slightly.

My hand covers my mouth, as if I'm trying to stop myself from saying the words.

Kadian is dead.

*

Shepherdstown had an official population of eight hundred, but if you counted the surrounding neighbourhoods it was more like two thousand. It had seven churches, a library, a town hall and a row of boutique shops. The campus of a small college was set a few yards off the main street.

Our house was located in the town centre, two blocks from the campus. In Shepherdstown, I soon learned that everyone knew your business. And everyone was surprisingly friendly. Shortly after we arrived, I walked down to the bakery for a cup of coffee. I was distracted, thinking about the renovations which were going to take longer than we had expected. 'You seem in a bad mood,' the young lady behind the counter said.

'Pardon?' I replied, flustered.

'You just seem a little down, that's all. Perhaps this coffee will pick you up.'

I said nothing. Paid for the coffee and left, feeling irritated. What cheek! But then I thought about it. She had sounded genuine. Perhaps it was a positive thing. I smiled. It was the first of many cultural epiphanies I would have during my stay in the USA.

As we had done before, Deb and I continued to share the child-care fifty/fifty. When I was on duty, I would take the kids down to the library – a two-storey white-brick building which previously had served as the town's fire station. We would sit upstairs, in tiny wooden chairs, and I would read them one, two, three books. 'Another, another,' they would cry as soon as I had finished.

After reading, we'd visit the bakery next door. Kadian and Sam would always order the same things: a small carton of chocolate milk and a chocolate doughnut with sprinkles on top.

Then we would walk around town. To the Town Run, a stone-walled river that cut across the main street. To the Rumsey Monument, a celebration of the first steam-powered boat, by a small park on the edge of the Potomac River. Or to the park itself, where we clambered over the climbing frame or twisted around on the swings.

The children's favourite place was the Little House, a tiny grey-stoned house filled with miniature beds, sofas, curtains and books. It was rarely open, but when it was, Kadian and Sam would go inside, play with the pots and pans in the kitchen, or run upstairs to the bedrooms. I would stand outside and watch them through the first-floor window.

When I wasn't taking care of the kids I was busy finding myself a new career. Deb and I had decided early on that we couldn't commute to Washington DC. I looked for film work in Shepherdstown, but there wasn't any. I tried to find a job at the local television station, but there was nothing available.

So I invested in real estate. We had a little money left over from the sale of our house in Oxford and, given that property prices were so low in West Virginia, I managed to make it go far. Before long I was managing a portfolio of single-family houses, apartment buildings and commercial units. Then I passed my real-estate exam and, without much thought, joined a firm of realtors. Soon I was driving clients around West Virginia in an enormous navy-blue Dodge pickup truck, showing off newly built McMansions and prime plots of land.

I knew I had become part of the American Dream when I pulled up to the drive-through of my local bank and, as I handed over a thick wad of five- and ten-dollar bills from my tenants, the young teller told me how much she liked my new truck.

My friends in England couldn't believe it when I told them that I had become an estate agent. 'Oh how the mighty have fallen,' they cackled at the end of the telephone line. I didn't care. We had enough money to get by, and could spend as much time with the kids as we liked. I began to make a list of the features I wanted in my next truck.

*

One week after the accident, a letter arrives from the police station in Wiltshire. It is lying on the doormat when I come down in the morning.

I am surprised that Duke didn't bark at the postman. He's been strangely quiet ever since our return, keeping himself to himself. Normally, he would pad up to one of us, every few minutes, for a nuzzle and a stroke. Now he spends most of the day just lying on his large pillowed bed, head between his outstretched paws, a sad lost look on his face. Is it possible that in some way he knows what has happened?

I pick up the envelope and tear it open. Inside are three copies of Kadian's death certificate, printed on cream-coloured heavy paper with a watermark two-thirds of the way up. They have his name slightly wrong, Kadian Cackler-Harding. There should be no hyphen between the last two names. We had dropped the hyphen years before and registered the name change in a West Virginia courtroom, but the information had clearly never made it to the English legal system. The document stated that Kadian had died on 25 July 2012. The cause was 'trauma to the brain'.

I am holding Kadian's death certificate. Strength drains from my legs. I sit down on a chair in the hallway. It is like being told that he has died for the very first time.

After a few moments I look through the other papers in the envelope. There is a generic twelve-page pamphlet entitled 'How to Deal with Grief'. I flick through the pages, and toss it in the rubbish bin.

*

Kadian saw his first dolphin on a beach in South Carolina when he was six years old.

There were three of them, diving in and out of the surf, less than a hundred feet from the shore. He just stood there and watched, transfixed. By the time we got back to Shepherdstown he had researched and memorised their basic physiology: pectoral fins to change direction, dorsal fins to provide stability, the fluke tail to propel them through the water. He learned the differences between a bottlenose and a melon-headed dolphin, an Amazon River and a Yangtze River dolphin. Together we discovered that dolphins use sonar to navigate through the ocean depths, that they speak to each other through a series of clicks, that they are one of the most intelligent creatures on earth.

Until he was twelve or so, whenever he was happy, he would

hold his elbows to his sides, raise his forearms up to his chest and, with his wrists hanging close together – like two pectoral fins – he would make an 'ak-ak-ak' sound.

For his birthdays, and on many other occasions as well, we visited the National Aquarium in Baltimore, Maryland, which was only a short drive from where we lived in West Virginia. There we were wowed by the seahorses and the alligators, the terrapins and the clownfish. But the main attraction, the reason for our visit, was the afternoon dolphin show. We'd arrive early to get seats in the 'splash zone', and excitedly watched dolphins jump for bright orange balls, perform aerial acrobatics and thwack their fins against the water, leaving us soaking wet.

On one visit we purchased two stuffed orcas – a mummy and a baby orca. Kadian explained to us that, despite being known as 'killer whales', they belonged to the ocean dolphin family. These two joined his other little friends that lived on his bed: a tortoise hand puppet, whose head went in and out of his shell, a black Labrador puppy, and a family of bottlenose dolphins (mama, papa and baby). But the orcas were his favourite. From that day on, he used Mummy Orca as his pillow.

After the show we walked downstairs to look through the glass walls of the giant holding tanks. Kadian put his nose to the window, 'ak-ak-ak,' he called. 'Ak-ak-ak.' It is unlikely that the dolphins heard – no sound could have penetrated the three inches of glass – but almost immediately one of the dolphins swam directly up to him, blue snout against pinkish nose, hovering there, looking into Kadian's eyes. Giggling with pleasure, Kadian continued his 'ak-ak-ak' until, after three or four minutes had passed, the dolphin turned and glided away.

It was Kadian's first obsession. He read everything he could on dolphins, sat transfixed through countless wildlife documentaries and watched *Free Willy* repeatedly. I found two seasons of the 1960s TV show *Flipper* on eBay and, on special occasions, I would give him a video cassette, each cover adorned with smiley suntanned boys and fin-waving dolphins.

I started calling him Flipper, which slowly turned into Flops. As in 'Good morning, Flops', or 'How was your day, Flops?' I was the only one to call him this. A five-letter word that summarised the long history of rich and complex father–son moments.

There were other unique connections. But it was always Flops, used in moments of tenderness and vulnerability, that was our thing. Our bond.

*

The phone rings every few minutes. People pick it up and speak in soft tones. I am never offered the receiver; I don't want to talk to anyone.

'Does everyone know?' I ask. The idea of talking to people on the telephone about what has happened exists on the other side of some imaginary line that I have erected. I am sitting on the sofa, coping, just about. Phone calls are over there, unapproachable, unthinkable.

'I called people.' Deb is sitting next to me, typing messages on her iPhone. 'I had five hours to wait for my plane,' she says. 'I have no idea who I called. In fact, I have no idea how I got to the airport. But I think I called everyone.'

'You called us,' says Jane from the kitchen. She is making dinner.

'What did I say?'

'You said that you had some terrible news. That Kadian had been hit by a van. And that you were still in America and that you needed me to be with Sam, as soon as possible. That I must act in your place, as the mother figure.'

Again I am amazed by the brain's ability to operate at a time of transcendent pain. How could Deb organise the care of her daughter, from thousands of miles away, when she had just been told that her son had died?

A doctor comes to see us. He gives us sleeping pills. This will be the second night after Kadian's death. We pull a futon into our room and make up a bed for Sam. We decide it's best if we stick close. Everyone leaves except for my sister Kate. We say goodnight.

I wake at around seven in the morning. Kadian is dead, my brain reminds me. Kadian is dead. I had forgotten. I start crying again. Deb is lying next to me.

'Is it real?' she asks. 'Is it really happening, Thomas? Has he really gone?'

I roll over and hold her. This is real. Our life is over.

We don't want to wake Sam, so we go downstairs. My sister is up. She makes us coffee and we sit on the sofa. Deb is whimpering. Tears are falling from my eyes without end. I am prone to crying, but I have never cried like this before.

'This can't be happening,' says Deb again. She starts to rock back and forth. She is wailing, heaving. We are home and it is finally safe. We hold each other. 'How can we live?' she asks Kate. 'How can we live?'

Kate is crying as well. 'I don't know how,' she says. 'But you will. You will. You have Sam. You will find a way.'

I don't believe her. I don't think there is a way. We cannot live like this. The pain is too much. I miss him too much.

'Where is he?' I scream. 'Where is Kadian?' I want my son back. I am mad with it. I am mad with loss.

*

Kadian's love for animals grew. His new bedroom slowly became a sanctuary for reptiles and rodents. There was Gandalf the tree frog, a hamster named Panda, two geckos, whose names I cannot remember, and Speedie the lizard. The hamster was easy to look after, but the reptiles ate only crickets, which soon began to arrive by post, boxed in their thousands.

Kadian spent hours keeping his little friends company, cleaning their cages and tanks, making sure they had enough water, switching their heating lamps on and off. Whenever guests came to the house, whether young or old, he would take them upstairs to see his pets, patiently describing their characteristics, their habits, their likes and dislikes.

But despite Kadian's (and Deb's) constant care and attention, his pets had short lives. And with each passing, Kadian was inconsolable. Between the red-brick wall of our house and the white stucco of the house next door was a narrow pathway, bordered with an overgrown flower bed. Kadian and Sam told us that this would be the family graveyard, and carefully cleared it of leaves, rocks and weeds. Each time an animal died, we dug a tiny grave, wrapped the animal in cloth or placed it in a decorated box, put it in the hole, and said a few words.

When Speedie, the oldest and most beloved of the lizards, died, my cousin James was visiting. Kadian asked if he'd give a eulogy, and James took the matter very seriously, praising

Speedie for his long life of love and service, his months of dedicated cricket-eating, and for the joy that he had brought the family, and Kadian.

But it turned out that Kadian's greatest animal love was not to be the lizards, or hamsters, or dolphins, but dogs.

We had owned dogs before. First there was Molly the sheepdog, who had been a lot of fun but completely mad, and had been adopted by our builder, Marcus. And then there was Coco, the runaway black Labrador. We eventually found Coco a home on a farm just outside town, a fact that Kadian never quite believed.

But ever since our arrival in America Kadian had begged us for a dog. He researched the various breeds. He swore that he would be responsible for walking and feeding and training it. He even designed a PowerPoint presentation listing the benefits of canine ownership. It was very persuasive.

The next week, after seeing a sign for German shepherd puppies in a local coffee shop, we drove out to a small house near Harpers Ferry. In the garden we were quickly surrounded by six fluffy, bouncy, things, their ears flapping wildly, their paws far too big for their little bodies, their tails wagging with excitement.

One puppy caught Kadian's attention. Frisky like the others, yet docile, he allowed himself to be picked up and turned over without fuss. We were sold. Kadian asked what the puppy was called, 'His name is Duke,' said the owners. A few minutes later we were driving home with an envelope full of official paperwork and Duke asleep on Kadian's lap.

*

Kate's husband, Simon, joins us for lunch. After we have eaten we take our coffees outside and sit at the patio table. I ask him about the accident, about Kadian's injuries. Simon is an anaesthetist, with many years of experience treating victims of motorbike, car and bicycle accidents.

'I've been talking with my colleagues about it,' he says. 'Perhaps, if I had been there, I could have done something.'

His words cause the breath to catch in my throat. Dread floods my body. Is it possible that Kadian could have been saved? Would he still be alive if he'd had better medical attention?

'But the paramedics said they did everything possible,' I say, 'What would you have done?'

'That's the problem,' he says. 'I might have got him breathing, but it's almost certain that he would never have regained brain function. You would have been faced with the choice of allowing him to live in a vegetative state, or letting him die. I'm glad you never had to make that decision.'

I wonder for a moment if I agree. Would I have wanted that choice, with its sliver of hope that he may have recovered? But what would his life have been like?

These 'what ifs' are a slippery slope, and my mind quickly slides on to others. What if we had taken another route? What if I had cycled ahead of Kadian? What if he had gone to another bike store? What if . . .

I look back at Simon, forcing myself to change mental track.

'And what actually is brain trauma?' I ask. 'What actually happened?'

One of the great things about Simon is there is no bullshit. No sugar-coating. If I ask a question, he answers immediately.

'When Kadian hit the windscreen, or perhaps the road, his skull's movement through the air would suddenly stop, but the brain's movement would continue. It would have slammed against the inside of his skull causing massive trauma. It would have been instant.'

'So he would have felt no pain?' I hadn't realised that this had been troubling me, but as soon as I say the words I understand that his answer is critical.

'He wouldn't have felt anything. He would have lost consciousness immediately. He would have died on impact, if not very soon after.'

'I knew he was gone as soon as I saw his eyes,' I say. 'They were so wide, so still. He didn't look like Kadian at all.'

'That's a classic sign of brain death,' he says. 'It happens when the brain is cut off from the central nervous system.'

There it is. The medical description matches my experience. For now, at least, the descent down the well has been halted. I have found another little ledge on which to rest my body.

*

Duke was clearly Kadian's dog from the very beginning. Kadian fed him and took him on walks. He spent hours brushing him, pulling out clumps of hair as his coat adapted to the warmth of our house.

Around town, Kadian would introduce Duke to both friends and strangers. When people commented on his large paws he would explain that Duke would grow into them. When asked about his enormous ears that drooped against his head, Kadian would tell them that Duke did not have enough strength yet to hold them up, but in time, he would.

Soon, with the assistance of doggy treats, Kadian was teaching

Duke to sit, come and lie down. At the library, he borrowed books on German shepherds. 'Did you know, Daddy,' he said to me, 'that the English call German shepherds by a different name? They started calling them Alsatians after the First World War because they were so angry with the Germans.'

'Just like how the people in Shepherdstown changed German Street to Main Street,' I said.

'Exactly. And did you know that German shepherds are the third most intelligent dog, after the Poodle and the Border collie?' he said, without pausing for breath. 'And did you know that they use German shepherds as police dogs and rescue dogs because they are so smart and strong? And did you know . . .'

And so it went on.

*

After lunch we agree to walk up to the Poet's Stone that stands on top of Shoulder of Mutton, the oddly named hill behind our house. Ours is a small village, made up of a hundred or so houses, a village hall and two pubs. The poet Edward Thomas lived in a stone cottage just up the road from us. Every day he walked up the steep slope behind the village to his writing studio at the top of the hill.

I am chilled before we even leave the house. On top of my jacket I wrap myself in a blanket. I have no strength in my legs. Kadian and I have walked up this hill hundreds of times. It is hard work, but I have never failed to climb it.

Slowly we walk along the road, and then left onto Mill Lane, where a memorial stands to those who died in the First World

War. Nobody comments on my pace, they adjust their stride, we stay as a close group.

At the waterfall at the bottom of the hill we enter a gravelly trail. I am walking slower now. We pass a hollowed-out heart-shaped tree stump where a few months earlier I had taken a photograph of Kadian and Sam – I cannot look at the tree today. I stumble. Sam holds my arm.

We cross a small lane, walk through a muddy field, and then we are at the foot of the final slope. From here I know that it climbs precipitously. I am not sure I can do it. Sam walks next to me, holding my arm, encouraging me, singing to me as we place one laborious step after another. I have to rest frequently to catch my breath. I feel like an old man.

Finally we make it to the top. I walk up to the large round stone that is planted in the turf, touching it to confirm my arrival. On the stone is attached a brass plaque with a line from Edward Thomas: '*And I rose up and knew that I was tired and continued my journey.*'

I collapse on the ground still panting. Normally I would have taken a few moments to enjoy the view of the valley between Shoulder of Mutton and the South Downs. But not today. While the others talk in hushed tones, I pull the blanket tight around me and fall asleep.

*

When Kadian turned seven I taught him how to ski.

The mountains are in our blood. My father's family comes from Switzerland and Germany and the love of winter sports,

Alpine peaks and *glühwein* has been passed down from generation to generation. From Shepherdstown it was too expensive and time-consuming to fly to Europe's romantic resorts or the deep powder slopes of the Rockies. But we had something far better: Whitetail ski resort, Pennsylvania.

I declared Tuesdays to be 'ski days'. As soon as it became cold enough, in early December, I would pick Kadian up from school and we'd drive straight to the slopes. By the time we arrived it would be dark and bitterly cold. But it didn't bother us. This was night skiing – the nursery slopes illuminated by piercing white lights, the runs coated with the soft padding of man-made snow.

Kadian instantly fell in love with skiing, and picked it up quickly. Bored by the nursery slopes he nagged me to try the red runs which were both steeper and longer. After a couple of ski-school lessons I gave in, nervously skiing behind him, shouting instructions as he snowploughed down.

Though the slopes were relatively quiet at this time of day, there was enough traffic to cause concern. Snowboarders were the worst. They would frequently careen down the mountain, out of control, crashing into anyone who got in their way. I taught Kadian to stick to the sides of the piste as a precaution, and would ski behind him to absorb the hit, if there was one. Sometimes, when the coast was clear, I would ski backwards in front of him, my ski tips pointing up the slope, and from this vantage point I could see his face, enthralled, wide-grinned, concentrating, often giggling. 'Whoop, whoop, whoop,' I'd ululate, 'you're doing great, Kads, you're doing great!'

After ten or so runs, our legs aching, our faces stinging with the cold, we would head to the lodge to take a rest. Hands wrapped around steaming mugs of hot chocolate, we would sit at a table next to one of the large windows facing the slopes, watching the other, hardier, skiers glide, and twist and *schuss* their way down the mountain.

After a while, now warmed up, one of us would say that it was time to hit the slopes again. With mock weariness we would pull on our ski boots, jackets and gloves, and head out of the lodge. If we were lucky, we could grab another ten runs before we would have to drive back home. After all, there was school tomorrow.

Even better than the skiing were the lift rides between the runs. We'd hop onto the swift-moving chairlifts and sit close, bodies touching, keeping warm. If we were unlucky enough to be caught in a blizzard billowing from one of the snow machines, we tucked our heads down, woollen hats touching, laughing like two hardened sailors in a storm. Or if we were stuck on the lift, because some fool had failed to get on properly, bouncing up and down on our chair like sedentary bungee jumpers, we would dare each other to lick the frigid metal, fearful that our tongues would stick, or click our skis together, flicking snow into each other's faces. Or we would laugh at the incompetence of skiers beneath us, or marvel at others as they gracefully hopped around moguls. Or, and these were the very best moments, my most cherished memories, we would just sit perfectly still in our chair, dangling from the thick metal cable swaying in the freezing air, blanketed by the silence of the cloudless night sky, filled with a million brilliant stars, the view of the distant valley dotted with little houses, illuminated by the moonlight above. We were one, together, huddled close, father and son.

'This is so beautiful,' Kadian would say.

'I'm so glad we're here together,' I'd reply.

And then we would hear the distant rumble of the motor starting up, the cable jerking overhead, and we would move forward again.

PART II

I lose track of the days.

Our house fills with people, empties and fills again. Family members, friends, neighbours, parents of Kadian and Sam's school friends, teachers from their school. Flowers arrive, from London and the USA.

Charlie, Debora's boss and very close friend, drives into town and prints twenty or so photographs of Kadian. When he gets back, we put the pictures in frames and build a shrine in front of the fireplace. Debora adds votive candles, Kadian's iPhone and a large bar of Cadbury's milk chocolate. It's a beautiful, poignant sight.

Food is cooked, eaten and cleared up. I am in a daze. I don't know what to do with myself. Deb, Sam and I agree that every two hours we will retreat to our bedroom to reconnect. To try and perform our roles as grieving parents and sister even if we do not yet know what these roles are.

A crate of whisky is purchased. It is drunk within a couple of days. Someone buys another. We stay up late and finish the packet of sleeping pills sooner than we thought we would. Before I might have worried about it. Not now. I take the pills. I want the sleep. The escape.

Soon we run out of room. There are so many friends who have come to be with us. We are saved by our neighbours, who invite our guests to stay. These small details remind me that this is not just another death, someone loved who has now passed on, but an event significant enough for people to drop everything and travel halfway across the world to be here, for strangers to open their doors. It is not that I need reminding – my heart is broken, my mind crazed – but these things are reassuring. I am going mad for a legitimate reason.

*

Kadian's passion for chocolate started early. I believe I can pin it down exactly, to his first taste of chocolate ice cream in a small cafe off the main square in Siena, Italy, at the age of six months. It was a shock to his system, this combination of sugar, cream and chocolate. His eyes dilated, his tongue hovering in mid-air post-lick, it was almost possible to see his synapses dancing with delight.

Soon after we arrived in Shepherdstown, Deb and I took Kadian and Sam to have lunch at the Old Pharmacy Cafe, a family-friendly diner in town. We ordered burgers, fries and milkshakes.

It was one of those old-fashioned places where they delivered the milkshake in a tall glass and the remaining mixture in a metal mixing cup. Kadian drank the contents of both containers and promptly threw up on the restaurant table.

For most people, this would have been a lesson. Not so to Kadian. More was always better.

At parties, he would eat as many biscuits and sweets as he could, never in a mean, selfish way – there wasn't a mean bone in his body – but in a let's-see-what-I-can-get-away-with way. At Halloween, he would collect a pillowcase full of sweets, and eat the contents within twenty-four hours.

Deb and I shared our concerns about this behaviour on a few occasions. Might it be a sign of an addictive personality? Or did he just live for the moment, a lover of the good things in life?

We decided it would probably be the latter. At restaurants, aged ten, he would ask for the biggest, most expensive steak on the menu. When I asked him why – trying to send a parental message about frugality – he would simply answer, 'Because it's delicious.'

*

The day after Kadian's death Deb posted a message on Facebook:

> My dearest of friends. It is with the deepest core of my broken heart that I alert you all of Kadian's death yesterday. He was the happiest child he could have ever been. He had his new bicycle and was on a ride with Thomas and four others when a van hit him full on. That beautiful spirit of his was whisked away from us immediately. He had the best week of his life – having just finally built the tree house of his dreams, built a new bike, and obtained a ticket

> to come in and set up 27 iMacs for the new computer network at City Bikes in Washington DC for a special Mum/Kadian time. The Apple Business Center were so impressed with him that they were going to train him. 14.5 years of a perfect child. What a strange thing to announce the death of our child on Facebook but Kadian would have approved.

If I was more present, more aware, more sensitive, perhaps, I might have stopped her. If she wasn't overwhelmed by grief she might not have posted it. But the result is pure magic. Since that post, Facebook has played a key role in our lives. With it, we are able to instantly connect with our many family and friends around the world, and more importantly, hear from them how Kadian's sudden death has affected their lives.

In Shepherdstown, West Virginia, three of Kadian's friends organise a candlelit vigil outside our old house. Over one hundred people stand in the pouring rain, reading poems and remembering stories.

In Washington DC, staff at Deb's store arrange a bike ride to the city's key Kadian locations: the White House, the Lincoln Monument and the Apple store.

In Vietnam, a candle is lit and sent on a small boat down a river. Another is lit on a cliff overlooking the sea in Cape Town. Another is lit in Paris, another in Delhi.

Knowing that over a thousand people are with us, are going through this together, on a day-by-day, hour-by-hour level, gives us extraordinary strength. It is as if we are being physically held up by a large group of people.

But despite the support, the messages, the network of friends and loved ones, I cannot function. For I am no longer an individual, with a sense of self or perception of where my physical and mental boundaries are. It is as if I have lost my outer shell and I merely flow into the rest of humanity, the rest of the universe. I am now functioning at a very low amoeba-like level. I can just about feed myself, relieve myself and sleep, but little more. I could no more organise a trip to the supermarket to purchase provisions than fly a 747 jet plane. This is more than being in a daze, it is a total lack of higher-level brain capacity.

I try to explain to people that my world is no longer reliable or predictable. One moment I was cycling through the countryside with my family, happy, free-wheeling through the sunshine, without any sense of threat or fear, and then, suddenly, without warning, he is gone, my son is dead.

How can I operate in a world like this? In which I cannot predict what will happen if I pursue a certain course of action. I am no longer certain that the roof will not fall on my head or that the ground will remain firm under my feet. As such, it is impossible for me to function. This is not a rational choice, this is my new instinct, my new reflex.

They nod, touch my arm in sympathy, hug me. But I know they don't understand, not really. Their world remains predictable, reliable. They can leave our house, get in their car, and return home without expecting their universe to fall apart. I see them with their children, and I become jealous. I want their lives, I want their ease, their lack of concern. Everything that has been torn from me. I refill our glasses and we drink more whisky.

My son is dead. Kadian is gone. Nothing else matters.

*

In 2007 Hillary Clinton came to Shepherdstown on a campaign trail before the West Virginia primary. It was a big deal for our small town. We didn't receive many famous visitors.

Excited by the prospect of the first female president, Debora supported Hillary. Sam, following her mother's lead, also wanted Hillary to win. Kadian supported Obama. He liked his style, he was excited by his progressive politics, he was inspired by his story. I couldn't make up my mind, and was sitting on the fence.

On the day of Hillary's visit, Sam and I walked to the rally carrying Hillary signs, and Kadian carried one for her opponent. We arrived early, the candidate was late. We waited and waited on the steps of the McMurran Hall, a large yellow-stoned building in the centre of our town.

After three hours we were exhausted and bored. Behind us a crowd of five hundred people stirred restlessly. A campaign worker approached Kadian. She said, 'Son, if you want to be up here you can't have that sign.' She took away his sign and replaced it with one of Hillary's. He was too tired to complain.

Instead, he sat on the ground, cross-legged, white cap askew on his head, clutching the bars of the crowd control barrier as if it were a cage. A photographer squatted down and took a picture of him, and it was this picture – not that of Hillary speaking to the crowd or happily signing their upturned palms – that was later distributed on the news, and printed in the *Wall Street Journal*, *USA Today* and many other papers around the world. In the end, his support for Obama had been communicated.

*

I wake up screaming. Deb is next to me, also screaming. It's eight in the morning. I have just woken up and remembered that Kadian is dead. Is this really happening? How is that possible? Where is he? Why is he gone?

Sam comes in. We have woken her up. This is more than I can bear. We are being so selfish, yet how can we not be? How can we not scream and shout? She says that she perfectly understands our need to shout and scream, but could we please wait till after nine in the morning? Her precocity and grace cheer me up. We promise her that we will do our best, and she returns to her bedroom.

I go downstairs. Nobody is up yet. There are ten people sleeping in the house, ten others staying in the village. I am glad that the kitchen is empty. I make some coffee, sit at the table by myself; the silence of the morning echoes in my head.

I make a list of things to do:

Find funeral parlour
Tell police we are ready to pick up Kads
Burial site or crematorium?

We have some decisions to make. The hospital wants to discharge Kadian's body as soon as possible. We need to find a place for him to stay, allow people a chance to see him one last time. Should we have a burial or a cremation? I haven't been to many burials. The argument in my family has been that you don't want to burden your children with having to visit your grave. I think of this and groan. Another reminder that Kadian's death is not 'right'. Burial then. But where? I don't want anything formal, a creepy graveyard, a mahogany coffin, some weird mock-Victorian Gothic memorial service with dark wooden benches and men in top hats. Was there an alternative? I had never heard of one.

I struggle to focus. I am used to working under pressure, to multitasking. Project management is the oxygen I breathe. Not today. I am overwhelmed and tired just thinking of these questions. As soon as I begin to tease out some of the nuances – how would I feel about others seeing Kadian's body? What do I want a service to look like? Who should attend? – my brain shuts down. I don't want to go there. I just want to sleep.

Deb joins me in the kitchen. I show her the list. She is much clearer. She wants a natural burial. She remembers hearing about a place located less than ten miles away, on the South Downs. She makes a phone call and arranges a visit for later that day.

My sister Amanda walks into the kitchen a few minutes later. She suggests that she and Jane take over the logistics, particularly the locating of a funeral home and the liaising with the police. 'We'll keep you in the loop the whole way,' she says. 'We won't make any decisions without you.' I feel relieved and thank her.

I wander into the living room and lie on the enormous sofa we brought back from America. Its back is made of solid walnut, its coarse fabric adorned with ripe paisley-type golden flowers. Its cushions are plump, oversized and edged with tassels. Kadian and I watched television on this sofa. We threw cushions at each other and wrestled on this sofa. On one of its burgundy leather wings Kadian had scratched his initials: K.H.

I close my eyes, waiting, while unwanted images flicker through my brain.

*

Seven months after Hillary Clinton's visit to Shepherdstown, we rose early and took a bus to Washington DC.

It was 20 January 2009 and we were on our way to the inauguration of Barack Obama, the first African–American president of the USA. A few weeks earlier I had contacted the office of Robert Byrd, the senior senator from West Virginia, and they had sent us some tickets.

After waiting in line to clear security, we hurried ahead, wanting to get the best possible view. We were lucky. After hustling through the crowds, we managed to squirm our way to the very front. The only thing that stood between us and the podium where President Obama would stand were the rows of chairs laid out for foreign dignitaries and members of Congress.

Behind us, over a million people were gathered, clutching cups of coffee in gloved hands, glancing at the giant television screens, shouting Obama's name. And then there he was, we could see him clearly.

'Thank you, thank you, thank you,' shouted Obama to the crowd.

'Obama, Obama, Obama,' they shouted back.

Then someone called out 'Shhh'. The crowd was silenced.

> On this day, we gather because we have chosen hope over fear, unity of purpose over conflict and discord [applause] . . . know that America is a friend of each nation and every man, woman and child who seeks a future of peace and dignity, and we are ready to lead once more [applause] . . . To those who cling to power through corruption and deceit and the silencing of dissent, know that you are on the wrong side of history, but that we will extend a hand if you are willing to unclench your fist [applause]

I looked over at Kadian. Keenly listening, engaged, focused, he clapped his hands at the end of each applause line. This was his president, talking about his world, his future.

A few weeks later Kadian wrote an essay about the inauguration. He explained how he had taken many photographs of the event but that he had lost the camera, so he would describe the day as a series of photos.

> Photo 1: My German shepherd Duke was sleeping next to my parents. He didn't know yet, but he was the only one that wasn't going.
>
> Photo 2: We were lucky to get seats because that bus was P-A-C-K-E-D to the max! It was so full and hot that I felt sick. Just as I thought I was about to throw up we finally came to a stop. Everybody streamed out of the bus into the beautiful but terrifyingly cold day.
>
> Photo 3: While I was on the bus I remembered Hillary Clinton came to my home town . . . I hoped that waiting for President Obama would not take so long.
>
> Photo 4: This was one of the biggest events in the history of the United States, and it was planned like the organisers paid less attention to crowd control than they did to Michelle Obama's wardrobe.
>
> Photo 5: Senator Byrd, Thank you so so so so so so so so so much for the tickets to the inauguration! We were right at the front of the purple section, perfect spot! We had a great time. When President Obama came out, everybody shouted so loud you would think that people could hear it back in West Virginia! It was such a great experience. I cannot believe that I was actually there! I will remember it for the rest of my life!

At the end of the essay Kadian wrote: 'Senator Byrd is interesting, because when he was younger, he was part of the hate group the Ku Klux Klan. And yet, he was one of the first people to endorse Barack Obama. This proves how far both he and this country have come. I am sad that I lost all of my camera photos, but I am glad to have the photo memories that will last for ever.'

Kadian was encouraged by his teachers to submit the essay to the West Virginia Writer's Contest for elementary school children. To his surprise, he won.

*

Deb and I are sitting on the sofa in our living room when Amanda walks in. Crouching down, she puts a hand on Deb's knee and says, 'I have good news about Kadian. He is arriving in Petersfield this afternoon.'

Deb convulses. For a brief, mad moment, she thinks that Kadian is coming home, alive. What other good news could there be? But no. I am devastated for my wife, for the high and low, and for my sister, who is trying her best. There is a lot of this during this period. People trying to say the right thing but getting it wrong.

'Sam is now an only child' (of course she isn't, she had a brother who has now died); 'Things will improve with time' (how do they know? And if things get better, does that mean we will forget Kadian, and our grief?); 'Do you think it was a good idea to let him cycle at the front of the group?' (my guilt, my darkest secret, my deepest pain); 'Are you feeling better?' (do they think that this is like a cold?)

I have no sympathy. At the very least, I think ungenerously, they can make an effort and deliver the right words. We are the ones who have lost our son, all they have to do is be sensitive. But I know this is mean-spirited, ungrateful, unhelpful.

*

When we first arrived in West Virginia someone told us that because the wages were so low and inconsistent we would need to work many jobs if we wished to survive. By 2009 I had four. I'd taken over the real-estate firm that I had been working in. I managed a portfolio of my own properties. As if that was not enough, along with two friends, I purchased a local monthly newspaper, and now spent much of my time interviewing politicians and writing articles. And I was also a dad.

I had to become a proficient multitasker, able to talk on the phone while emptying the dishwasher and making the kids' breakfast. Able to walk the dog, while helping one of the kids learn their lines for a play, while picking up mail from the post office and delivering a signed contract to a client who lived down the street. Life was stressful, but I loved it.

At this time we were home-schooling Kadian and Sam. We could work and play when we wanted. We took the kids to Washington DC for piano lessons at the Levine School of Music, and for visits to the Air and Space Museum and the Modern Art Museum. We formed a history group with other home-school families and built a massive pyramid out of straw bales to learn about ancient Egypt. We spent two months in Europe, visiting the Colosseum in Rome, the Eiffel Tower in Paris, the Crown jewels at the Tower of London. It was all fun, all educational. We knew that we were very fortunate.

Not everyone approved of our lifestyle. Some of our family members asked us if we were sure we were doing the right thing. Weren't we damaging the kids' chances of getting into top universities, of having successful careers? Wouldn't they become social nerds? Was home-schooling even legal? We just told them that it felt right, at least for now. We were lucky to be able to spend so much time with them.

After two years, however, Sam said that she had had enough. She wanted to spend time with other children her age. Kadian went along with the plan. Soon they were attending Powhatan, a large school in Virginia, where they were taught trigonometry, the habits of homework and to raise your hand if you needed to go to the bathroom.

We now had to make packed lunches each day, which I hated. The kids quickly became bored with my cucumber and cream-cheese sandwiches and ziplocked bags of pretzels. Every morning I drove the kids to a mattress outlet store on the outskirts of town where a yellow school bus picked them up. I was on my own for the rest of the day.

*

We are forming a plan, slowly.

Deb, Sam, James, Charlie and I pile into the car and drive up to the Sustainability Centre near East Meon. Based in an old naval base at the top of the Downs, the centre is heavily wooded, and sits alongside the South Downs Way, a footpath that runs for a hundred miles from Winchester to Eastbourne. There is a three-storey red-brick building near the entrance, with a workshop on the first floor, vegetarian cafe and offices. The site runs courses in willow-fence weaving and pizza-oven building, among others, and hosts several events a year: a green festival in the spring, an 'uncivilisation' conference in August, a 'decluttering' workshop in September.

We are met by the director of the burial site, Al. He is a middle-aged man with curly grey hair, a wide smile and a rugged, seen-it-all demeanour. He gives us a tour of the place. The woods are full of ash, maple and beech, with scraggly juniper bushes growing underneath. Wild strawberries dot the chalky soil. There are no headstones. The only sign that there are dead bodies buried are the modest grey mounds that randomly appear throughout the site. I am surprised to find it so natural, unblemished, calming.

Al shows us an open muddy slope. 'This is the new section,' he says. 'We should be able to find a spot here.' It looks desolate to me, as if recently clear-cut. Only a few trees are left. Is this really where we want to bury him? I worry. I ask him if there are any other sites available. How about the more overgrown section we had walked through before? He thinks for a minute, and says there might be one. My hopes rise, I feel a surge of adrenalin. How surprising, I think to myself, that I could be excited about being offered a gravesite for my dead son, that there is still room for a sliver of positivity.

We trudge up through a small wooded area. 'It's over here,' Al points. In between a large oak, a couple of sturdy beech trees and a maple sapling, is a flat area of chalk and dirt. 'We had a cancellation this week. This is the last plot left in the old section.' I kneel down, and see wild strawberries in the ground cover. I pick three, give one to Deb, one to Sam, and eat the third. Above, the canopy opens to reveal a crystal-blue section of sky.

'He would have loved it here,' says Deb. 'He loved the woods, climbing trees. This will be like Kadian's very own campsite.'

*

It was Charlie who taught us how to camp. Typically unshaven, with long curly hair and a mischievous grin, Charlie was always introducing us to new things. To the kids he was something between a brother, an uncle and a pirate. We saw him every other weekend.

One Saturday morning, Charlie had driven up from Washington DC on his 1970s black BMW motorbike and announced that we were going camping. He had already booked a spot at his favourite site on the Shenandoah River, just south of Front Royal, Virginia. We began packing: tents, sleeping bags, canoes, kayaks, paddles, collapsible camp chairs, bright yellow blown-up inner tube, camping stove and a twenty-gallon water drum (there was no potable water at the site). We picked up food at a supermarket along the way.

It really wasn't a campsite, it was a 300-acre family farm owned by a woman called Brenda. For years she had allowed a select few to spend their weekends here. Turning the final corner of the dirt road that led into the campsite I was startled by the open valley, the towering ridge of the Blue Mountains, the wild grandeur. There were fourteen spots in all, approximately two hundred yards apart, each large enough to host up to twenty people. The sites were spread along the edge of the Shenandoah

River next to a large water meadow filled with a herd of ill-tempered black cows who liked to pay the campers a visit once in a while. This was camping in the raw.

We set up at number 7, a superb flat spot, with its own sandy beach and rope swing, well away from the adjacent sites. Sam efficiently erected her tent, I did the same for mine and Deb's tent, Charlie helped Kadian put up a hammock, and then strung up his own.

Kadian went off in search of wood and came back with a pile of kindling. Soon we had a raging fire. As the flames burned, Charlie peeled the bark off a couple of long sturdy sticks and skewered a couple of chickens. He then lowered these onto two upside-down Y-shaped sticks, buried into the ground. Deb and I shucked a bag of corn cobs and, having wrapped them in foil, laid them on a wire-mesh grill at the side of the fire. With dinner set to slow-cook, it was time to take a dip in the river.

Charlie tied the inner tube to the tree and before long he, Kadian and Sam were knocking each other into the water as each attempted to get onto the tube, their laughter and screams echoing off the cliffs on the other side of the river. After a while, Charlie returned to the fire and the kids wandered off to build a series of dams at the river's edge.

With the sun disappearing behind the ridge, it quickly grew dark and cold. We gathered around the fire, our swimsuits dripping into the camp chairs, towels wrapped around our shoulders, happily munching on crispy chicken and charred sweetcorn.

An hour or so later, when it was pitch black, Kadian said that he wanted to go skinny-dipping. Part shocked, part awed by his precocity, I said I would go too, though I was a little nervous of slipping on the rocks in the dark. I followed him into the water, my eyes adjusting to the near total absence of light away from the fire.

'Look at the fireflies, Dad,' he said, 'like a million rays of light.'

He was right. The entire riverscape was filled with dashing trails of golden yellow, burning bright against the cliff side's blackened face. We splashed around in the cool water until our limbs were numb. 'I'll get out first,' he said, not wanting me to see him naked. His self-consciousness had started a couple of years earlier. Just like learning to talk, riding a bike, his first day at school, it was another step on his path to manhood.

Before long we were all tucked into our sleeping bags, exhausted by the day's activities. Sometime deep into the night, perhaps around two or three, a peal of thunder exploded around our little valley. I was suddenly awake. Flashes of lightning tore through the night sky, carving instant shadows on our tent. I could hear Sam in the tent next to me, moving around.

'Are you OK, Sam?' I asked.

'I think so,' came her soft, uncertain reply.

Then the rain came. It felt like a bathtub-load of water was dumped every thirty seconds. Our little tent was barely able to withstand the pounding. And Kadian was still in the hammock, braving it under a tiny flysheet.

Deb and I quickly agreed that she would keep Sam company in her tent and I would make way for Kadian. 'Kadian, come and join me,' I shouted into the rain. I heard nylon being unzipped then the splash-splash of small feet in puddles. He dived through the small opening in my tent. 'Where's Duke?' he asked. I pointed to a simpering heap in the corner. Duke had joined us as soon as the rain had started. Leaning forward to give Duke a pat, I realised he was sitting in a large pool of water – the tent wasn't quite so watertight after all. We lay there for a while, Kadian, Duke and I, listening to the rain lash our tent, the trees moaning in the window, the boom of the now distant thunder.

'Five best things?' I asked. This was our goodnight ritual. Something we asked each other every night. And we lay there, snuggled close in the storm, naming everything that had happened to us that day. We quickly realised that five was not enough, and today we allowed the list to be extended to ten.

The next morning when I peeked out of our tent I saw that the campsite was flooded. The large canopy protecting our food supply had collapsed. A bag of bread, paper plates soiled with the previous night's dinner, various condiments and an empty bag of crisps floated in a muddy puddle. Towels and clothes that had been left out to dry hung sodden from a rope strung between two trees. And it was still raining.

'It's going to be a wonderful day,' said Kadian who was curled up next to me. 'At least it's warm.'

Putting on a hat, I stepped outside, retied the canopy over the food area, picked up some of the garbage, and fired up a small gas-powered stove. Soon we were all huddled under the canopy, drinking hot chocolate and munching on soggy granola bars.

There were pools of water everywhere. Kadian suggested that we drain the site, and before long we were racing to see who could dig a trench first from the campsite to the river. The slimy mud oozed through our toes, covered our hands and legs, making it hard to grip our shovels. We threw mud at each other, wiped it in each other's faces, running around the campsite, squealing with pleasure. And then, just as we completed the project, the rain stopped, the water sank into the soil, the trenches lay empty.

As we rested in our camp chairs, still giggling, Brenda drove up to our site. Taking one look at our earthworks, she shook her head, and commanded us to refill the trenches. Smiling and nodding, we said we would. Filling in would surely be as much fun as digging. And so we set to, Kadian leading the way.

Less than an hour later, the trenches were covered once again, and we were washing the dirt off our bodies in the river, the sun glittering on its gentle ripples, giant blue herons gliding overhead, and discussing how we would spend the rest of the day in this paradise.

*

A letter drops through our front door. It is a note from a couple who live a few doors down the road from us. They are both teachers at Kadian's school.

I had heard about Louise and Graham soon after our arrival in the village, a couple spoken of in slightly subdued tones: 'They lost their twenty-year-old son in India.' This memory comes back like a smack in the face. I can distinctly remember my own reaction: pity, sadness, curiosity, but most of all distance. My brain had filed the information into the 'happened to other people' folder. It is disconcerting to compare the memory of my own reaction to this couple against my current feelings, as if I was seeing myself from the inside and outside at the same time. Feeling a little ashamed at my previous lack of compassion, I wonder if this is how others feel about us. At the bottom of the note Louise and Graham have suggested that, if we want to, we should call, make contact.

A few hours later I am sitting in their small living room drinking wine. It is shocking to be in the same room as people who have also lost their son. Kadian's death feels so personal to me, so unique, so internal. But listening to their story, I realise that there are aspects we share: the sudden shock, the bewilderment, the wider family thrown into disarray, the problematic and sometimes hurtful way that people have spoken to us.

Watching Graham and Louise, I am struck by how they have given themselves permission to deal with grief in their own ways. Graham, the more introverted of the two, buries himself in work and rarely speaks of his son's death. Louise speaks of it often, visits his gravesite most days, finding solace in spending time with other parents who have lost their children. I think that this separate-but-together approach is both healthy and sensible.

But there is one comment that stands out. Louise has done most of the talking, generously sharing her pain and her attempts to live with it day-to-day. Suddenly Graham leans forward, wine glass in hand, and says, 'There was one thing I learned very early on that I found helpful. I was in India, having flown there overnight. I had just seen his body in the morgue. And I realised that this hurt, this anguish would be with me for ever. The only thing I could do was accommodate it.' Accommodate it. Not recover from it, or pass through it as one of a number of stages. This feels right. The heartache will always be there, I will have to learn to live my life with it, to grow around it, like a tree grows roots around a cold, inert boulder, always there, always present.

This feels right. I can do something with this.

*

Cycling was always a part of our family life. I had worked as a bicycle courier in London after I left school. Deb ran a chain of bike stores. We had met on a bicycle ride. When they were young, we pulled the kids around in a bicycle buggy. When they outgrew the buggy, we used it to pick up groceries. Kadian cycled to school each day. Sam's first big purchase was a bright red Italian racing bike. We went on long family bike rides together. Thirteen bikes were hanging in our shed. Bicycle posters adorned the walls of Kadian's bedroom.

One day, while we were walking around Shepherdstown, I told the children one of my favourite cycling stories, from the summer when Deb and I had cycled across the USA. It was a long, steamy afternoon, I recounted, and we had spent the past six hours steadily, exhaustingly, climbing a mountain in Colorado. It was massive. We must have climbed four thousand feet since breakfast. At the very top stood a Dairy Queen – an American ice-cream franchise. I was a little way ahead of Deb. I parked my bike on the lawn in front of the shop, walked inside and purchased a large double scoop of chocolate ice cream. It was cold, it was sweet, it was divine. A few minutes later, Deb walked in, exhausted, and asked if I could buy her a cone. She had run out of money. I refused.

'You are so mean!' Sam screamed.

'But I was only teasing,' I said. 'Your mother did worse to me.'

'But she would have been so hot, an ice cream would have tasted so good! You're a monster!' Kadian chimed in. After a few more minutes of professed shock at my behaviour, the subject was dropped. A few days later, Kadian bought himself a freshly baked chocolate-chip cookie from the bakery. I asked if I could have a bite, and he refused. 'Serves you right!' he said, laughing.

As they grew older, the kids spent more time on their bikes. Each year we built up their confidence and skills. Our rides stretched from five miles to ten, from ten to twenty, twenty to thirty. We invested in good bikes, lightweight with multiple gears, painted in bold colours. Now when they went out they wore black Lycra shorts and cycle jerseys.

Without doubt, the family's favourite ride was from Shepherdstown to Nutter's, the best ice-cream shop in the world. Not too short, nor too long, the route took us across the bridge that spanned the Potomac River, up a short hill, then along a five-mile stretch of perfectly smooth asphalt to the small town of Sharpsburg, Maryland.

Nutter's was open every day of the year, with the exception of Christmas and the Fourth of July, and I can never remember a day when there wasn't a queue of people waiting outside their doors. Once inside, we would be greeted by a kaleidoscope of flavours, with mouth-watering names such as Black Raspberry Blast, Bear Creek Caramel, Java Chunk and White Chocolate Truffle, Butterscotch, Cinnamon Chip and Blueberry and Cream. Behind the counter stood a line of women, their forearms robust from repeated scooping. With sweet pleading in their eyes, Kadian and Sam would ask me what size they could order. 'Small' was two massive scoops, 'Kiddy' was one enormous scoop. Normally I would stick to Kiddy, but occasionally, just to see their reactions, I would say, 'Go on, let's have Smalls today,' and I would be rewarded by an eruption of excitement and joy.

Kadian and Sam would typically order Cotton Candy, while I would opt for the more plebeian Chocolate Chip or Raspberry Ripple. We would go outside, sit on the stoop of one of the houses next door and, with great care and delight, lick our way to the bottom of our cones.

Then we would throw our napkins in the bin, remount our bicycles, and head away from Sharpsburg, past the great expanse of the Antietam National Battlefield, past the paddocks with ponies grazing, past a dairy farm with an ancient tractor and flagpole from which hung a massive red, white and blue flag, and down to the Potomac River, where we whooped and hollered, our minds ablaze with sugary wonder, as we made our way home.

*

I don't want to see him. I am not even sure what to call him: 'Kadian's body', 'Kadian's corpse', 'Kadian'.

What do you call the thing that looks like your son, your most precious son, but does not giggle when you tickle him or tell you that you're not funny when you make a joke? After some discussion, we agree to call him/it 'Kadian's body', making it clear that it is no longer Kadian, as he was, but also recognising that we are talking about more than an empty meaningless vessel.

We have similar discussions about other words and phrases. Each is fraught, carrying immense weight, as if we're inventing a new language. None of us like the word 'coffin' – it is too bleak, too heavy. Instead, we agree on 'burial basket', as the willow-woven container that he lies in looks like an oversized laundry basket. We feel strongly that 'funeral service' is wrong. We go back and forth, should it be a 'celebration', a 'memorial service', a 'burial'? In the end we agree on the slightly clumsy, but accurate, 'Celebration of Kadian's life and burial'.

Kadian's body is now at the local funeral parlour, and Deb has a found a sense of purpose. She informs me that she will stay with Kadian's body for the next forty-eight hours, until it is time to bury him. 'He came from me,' she says. 'I need to be with him at the end. I feel it is my responsibility as a mother.' This is both an explanation and a warning. The explanation: we are different, she is saying, we are both parents, but I am the mother, I gave birth to him, I am connected to him in a way that you can never be. And the warning: I am welcome to join her in this honourable task, but don't fucking mess with me, I am a lioness, I will not be stopped.

I experience a violent reaction to her words. This is the first time our instincts pull us in such different directions. There is no way on earth that anybody or anything is going to force me to spend time with my dead son's body.

Typically, I might put aside my feelings so that we can stay together, the need for companionship outweighing my personal preferences. I often stay up late just so that we can turn out the lights together, or I follow her round dusty museums in a foreign city despite feeling tired and bored. Yet right now this need to go through life side by side is not strong enough. Simply put, I do not want to spend time with Kadian's body.

However much I feel it, I am unable to articulate it. And no one spots my discomfort. Climbing into Jane and Greg's blue Land Rover, my legs heavy with reluctance, I mumble something about not being sure about going to the funeral home. 'We will be with you,' says Jane reassuringly from the front seat.

Also in the car is Sam. This is the first time that she will see her brother since the accident. There has been considerable debate between Deb and me as to whether or not this is a good idea. Her argument being that somehow seeing his corpse would add finality to the episode, it would provide something solid which Sam could refer to for the rest of her life.

Earlier in the day I scanned the Internet for evidence to back up her claim. In a study conducted two years after the Australian Granville train disaster in 1977, 61 per cent of those who had decided not to view the body of their relative or friend had subsequently regretted their decision, while those who viewed the body had better outcomes on a number of measures of psychological recovery than those who did not. Similarly, after the 1987 ferry disaster in the seas off the Belgian port of Zeebrugge, in which 193 people died, scientists concluded that those who viewed their relative or loved one's body were less likely to be distressed in the long term.

The counter-argument, put forward by myself, was that seeing her dead brother could be severely damaging. That she should remember him as he was, full of life. Never as a parent have I felt so ill-equipped to make a decision, one that could have such profound consequences. In the end, I am swept along by the others, painfully aware of my inadequacies, and my lack of backbone.

In Petersfield, we stop outside a flower shop. Deb wants to dress Kadian's room in the funeral home with plants and candles. She has brought along a sound system for her iPhone so that she can play music in the background. While the others are inside purchasing a basket of orchids, I remain alone in the Land Rover. I am trembling, terrified by what is coming; a flush of heat surges up my spine, my head becomes blurry and heavy, my heart races – I can feel the thud, thud, thud of its accelerated beat – blood pulses behind my ears. Am I experiencing a panic attack? A heart attack? Greg comes back to the car, asks if I am OK. 'I don't think I want to go to the funeral home,' I hear myself say, the words absurdly meek compared to the violence sweeping through my body. 'OK, bud,' he says. 'I'll run you home.'

I am selfish, weak, impotent, an unparent. I have lost one child and now I can't take care of the other. The rest of the group climbs back into the car and Greg drives me home. Before I close the door I tell them to call me if Sam needs help. A small part of my brain is still able to predict the possibility of future parental duties.

Entering the house from the side door, I avoid the people gathered in the living room, and walk upstairs. I close the curtains, crawl into bed and pull the duvet over my head, shutting out the world. I have never felt more pathetic, more lost. I am asleep in thirty seconds.

I am woken by my phone. It is Greg: 'Sam saw Kadian and she's very upset. She's collapsed on the floor. You need to come down here.'

Mechanically I leave my bed, put my shoes on and, walking downstairs, ask my friend Dominic to take me back into town. I check the clock – it is quarter past one. A few minutes later I am at the funeral home. The last place I want to be.

I see my sister-in-law Jen at the gate; I am not sure how she got here. She lives in Seattle. She looks grim. 'They're over there,' she says, pointing through a small courtyard to a side entrance. I open a door, then another, and look inside. Sam is on the floor, leaning against Greg, Deb is at the end of the room, looking down into a large wicker basket the size of a coffin. The room is lit by candlelight, and pictures of Kadian have been placed on a narrow shelf hanging from the wall. I am gripped by claustrophobia. I want to run, to resist the forward passage of time, which will inexorably lead to a lid being put on Kadian's basket, the final closure. When I will be unable to reach out, when he will be beyond my grasp.

'Hi, Sam,' I say. 'You want to get out of here?' She nods. I step into the room, help her up, and glance into the basket. Kadian is covered with the blue duvet that Deb has brought from his bedroom. His head is resting on Mummy Orca. I turn around and, half yanking, half hugging, walk Sam outside.

Once in the courtyard, Sam reassures me that she's fine. It was the right decision, she says. It was awful, but it was something she needed to do. And she is glad that it's over. 'I need an ice cream,' she says. That I can deliver, and we walk to the newsagent's round the corner.

Dom takes us home again. On the way I begin to wonder if I should intervene in my wife's plan. The burial is two days away. Is it sane to remain with Kadian in that small room? It strikes me as unbalanced, perhaps even obsessive. I am worried that Deb's grief has undermined her judgement. And yet, there is something about Deb's behaviour that seems natural, almost inevitable – a mother wanting to be with her son, to the very end. Having learned long ago that Deb is typically right, I decide to trust in her. I am thankful that Greg has offered to be with her, in the small room, for as long as she wants to stay.

I try to sleep but I can't. My brain is finding it harder and harder to make sense of the reality in which I live. I feel bewildered, separate from my surroundings. I am once again falling backwards down a blackened well.

Later that night, at around midnight perhaps, Deb and Greg return home. I go downstairs. They are carrying bags of candles and pictures. It has been an incredibly spiritual episode, Deb says. They had talked and talked, remembering special moments with Kadian. 'We were all together,' she says, 'the three of us. He was definitely in the room the whole time.' Then he changed. 'He no longer looked like Kadian,' she says with strength and calm, 'I wanted to stay longer but it was time to say goodbye.'

She tucked Kadian in one last time. With Mummy Orca still pillowed beneath his head and his blue duvet wrapped around his body, she kissed his right cheek, left cheek, chin and forehead, and then rubbed her nose against his. Then she stepped out of the room and told the funeral director that it was time to close the burial basket.

*

What is love?

The question has been asked so many times. Thousands of poems and songs have been written on the subject. Romantic comedies attract millions to cinemas. A comic strip ran for years starting, 'Love is . . .'

To me, this is love. This pain. This missing him. This aching need for him. This wanting to go back and have more of him.

I loved him the first moment I saw him. Pink and blue and funny-looking. I loved him when he towelled down his dog, wet from the rain. I loved him when he brought me a cup of tea on the sofa. I loved his narrow feet and thick brown hair. I loved looking at him.

It was both unreciprocated and reciprocated. It was a wanting to hold him, touch him, kiss him. And a letting go, allowing him to make mistakes, to forge his own way. It was the small things, like when he rose early and mowed a path through the field next to the village hall so he could walk to school without getting his shoes wet. And the big things, like when he painted RESPECT on his face in different colours, in solidarity with kids at school who were being bullied for being gay.

I still love him. But he can't love me back, and this tears my soul.

*

In 2004 we moved into the Old Firehall in Shepherdstown. It was a huge red-brick building that had been built in 1912 in response to a fire that had destroyed much of the town centre. At various points it had also served as the town hall, the town jail and the town's theatre.

Kadian liked to give tours to our guests. Starting in the basement where they had kept the old engines, he would describe the building's features: the firemen's bathroom with its stalls and urinal; the four-storey tower where the firemen dried the hoses; the twenty-five-foot-high pressed tin ceilings and the exposed brick walls; the lookout post where you could gaze over the entire town. We had converted one of the rooms into a mini-cinema, and here he would point out the swing seats salvaged from a cinema in Detroit and, best of all, the shiny red popcorn machine that he had been given for his birthday. He was an excellent tour guide. Visitors would comment on how mature Kadian was. More like a twenty-eight-year-old than an eight-year-old, they would say.

Saturdays were chocolate croissant days. 'I'm going to the

bakery,' Kadian would call up the stairs, 'do you want anything?' I'd shout down a request for a paper and two caffè lattes.

Kadian would pad back a few minutes later – without shoes or socks, as usual. This is the kind of town a kid should grow up in, I often thought, a town where it is safe to walk barefoot to the bakery to pick up breakfast, where you know that someone is always keeping an eye on the kids.

One Saturday, as he munched on his croissant, buttery flakes sticking to his cheeks, chin, nose – Kadian was the messiest eater I have ever met – he reminded me that it was the day of the May Day parade. 'Can I take Duke?' he asked.

I would guess that this parade was extraordinary even by American standards. There were the predictable fire vans dotted with yellow-helmeted volunteers, classic cars filled with beauty queens, and the school marching band, tossing batons, striding in step, plumed helmets quivering to the beat. But then there were the Morris dancers, marching alongside them, bells jangling on their legs, wooden staves smacking together. The Green Man strolled behind, recently plucked twigs dangling from his head, his face painted the colour of an overripe avocado, in his hand a large branch he used as a walking stick. Then the nursery children, pushed around in wheelbarrows like little wood elves. Perhaps, most astonishing of all, the Vestal Virgins – nubile late teens and twenty-somethings in flowing white dresses with flowers in their hair, dancing in circles down the streets. Finally came the dogs, dressed in bows and flowers, boaters and handkerchiefs, pulling along their smiling owners.

Kadian was in the middle of the pack, with Duke, who had a red ribbon tied to his collar, defying both his manhood and his pride, but neither boy nor dog seemed to care. Duke, god among dogs. A pure-breed German shepherd with the intelligence of a rocket scientist, the demeanour of an angel, the good humour of a talk-show host and the physique of a bodybuilder. Kadian, English kid, with a mop of brown hair, always giggling, an accent like Harry Potter's and a taste for all things sweet.

The pair strode down the road, peacocking their love for each other. The crowd cheered as they passed, 'Hey, Kadian,' called one of his friends. He turned and tossed some sweets in the caller's direction. Normally Kadian would have been the one scrabbling around scooping up sweets, but not today – not even sugar could trump being in the parade with Duke.

Later that afternoon, Kadian and Duke stood outside the town's Men's Club – today both men and women are members – lobbying people to vote for Duke to be put on the annual dog calendar, produced by the local pet store. 'Vote for Duke, he's the sweetest!' he called to those walking by, encouraging them to cast their ballot by handing out multicoloured lollipops – the lollipops had been Deb's idea; a long-time campaign organiser for politicians, she understood the dark arts of swaying voters – 'He's number 12.'

A couple of weeks later we received a call from the owner of the pet store. Not only was the photograph of Duke voted the best, he was so handsome and had received so many votes that she had decided to make him Mr January. Kadian couldn't have been more pleased.

'I told you he was the cutest,' he said to me, slurping from a spoon of chocolate cereal.

*

I frequently experience an exaggerated emotional response to the smallest things. It is both exhausting and overwhelming. It means that the safest, least emotionally taxing place is our bedroom, where I can hide from the tumult of unexpected and uncontrollable stimuli lurking in the outside world.

But even here, I am not always safe.

I am standing by the open window when the phone rings. 'Is Amanda Jennings there?' the young female voice enquires at the other end of the line.

'No, I'm afraid she's not,' I say. 'I think you have the wrong number. Who is calling?'

'I am looking for Amanda Jennings.'

'Yes, you said that. There is no Amanda Jennings here,' I reply, and hang up the phone.

A few seconds later the phone rings again. 'Hello, I'm looking for Amanda Jennings.'

'You just rang,' I say, more firmly, 'and I told you that she doesn't live here. Do you remember? Please don't call again.'

Another few seconds and the phone chimes again. 'There is no need to be so rude,' says the female voice. 'All I want to know is where I can find Amanda Jennings.'

'Look,' I shout, feeling the veins in my temples beginning to pulse, 'she does not live here! For the last time, stop calling us!'

As soon as I hang up the phone it rings again. I answer it and as I hear the first few words I pull my arm back and throw the phone as far as I can. It sails up, up, up, over the pond, through the top branches of a large oak tree, landing next to the hammock, a good fifty yards of telephonic flight.

For a few moments I feel guilty, embarrassed by my outburst. Then from across the pond, I hear the telephone ringing again. And I don't feel so bad any more.

*

My friend, let's call him William, has arrived at the house, uninvited.

Crowd control has become a constant concern: who can visit, when, for how long. The doorbell chimes, the phone rings, text messages ping. Our friends intervene. 'Do you want to speak to so-and-so?' they ask. I need to know who I will be spending the next few moments with, how these moments are likely to be filled – the big fear being that I will be asked open-ended questions, such as 'How are you doing?' There are only a few people who will let me be how I am, who can flex around my volatile, and often bizarre, emotional and physical state.

We are outside eating lunch on the patio when William walks through the French windows and joins us. 'Hello, everyone,' he says merrily. 'Looks like I'm just in time for lunch.'

I am sitting with Deb, Amanda, Jane, James, Sam and two others who have been with us from the start. They know the rhythms of our madness, they have learned how to talk with us so that we feel both listened to and guided, a very delicate balancing act. We have started our very first conversation about the burial arrangements. And no other topic is more difficult, more sensitive.

Jane has tentatively raised the question of timing. Should we hold the service in a day or two, or wait until the following week, to give us more time to prepare and allow people a chance to organise travel arrangements?

It is at this point that William arrives. 'It's customary to bury the body within three days,' he says, sitting down. 'That way it remains fresh. Have you thought about which rabbi you want present?'

The group looks at each other. By now we felt like brothers in arms, having endured the past days of insanity together. Here is this person, albeit a long-time friend, jumping into our process, telling us what to do, assuming decisions without sensitivity or discretion. I go inside, following my sister Amanda, who starts filling the dishwasher. I request that she ask William to leave. Two minutes later he is out of the door – his visit has lasted less than five minutes.

Back at the table we do a quick review of what has just happened. Seeking reassurance that I have been correct to eject William, I am told that given what we are going through, we can be as selfish as we like. This is not the time to think about other people's feelings. But it doesn't stop me from feeling guilty. Perhaps I have treated William too harshly. After all he has been a good friend, someone I've known since childhood, and he had travelled all the way from London to see us.

*

Every year, on the night of 31 October, over three thousand children dressed up as caped crusaders and zombies, white-faced femmes fatales and bedazzled pop stars, took to the avenues and alleys of Shepherdstown.

For their first few Halloweens, Kadian and Sam were eager to collect as much sugar-coated loot as possible from our neighbours. With pillowcases in hand they joined the throngs prowling the streets, dressed up in their own costumes: Kadian as Harry Potter with Sorting Hat, cloak and wand; Sam as a princess, with pink dress and sparkly tiara.

Then one year, we decided to organise our own event – a haunted house. We cleared the basement of clutter, and hung sheets of black shiny plastic from the ceiling, separating the room into a maze of tight corridors. With dim purple lights strung up, and eerie music playing from a portable CD player, the atmosphere was actually quite scary.

Sam and Deb drove to Washington to collect supplies from a toy store. When they returned Sam ran into the house to find me. 'Dad, you won't believe how much Mum spent!' she shouted. A few seconds later Kadian entered, laughing, carrying a large skeleton and a particularly nasty-looking werewolf mask. 'Isn't it exciting?' he said to me as he plopped his load onto the sofa, and turned to fetch the rest of the goodies from the car. 'This is going to be so much fun!'

We recruited a few friends to put the props to good use: a vampire who jumped out of an old trunk, a prisoner who was being electrocuted, and a doctor who hacked limbs from a screaming, blood-soaked patient. At six o'clock the haunted house was officially opened.

As they walked through the basement, our young, squeamish guests were startled by Kadian and Sam, who stood behind the black sheets squeezing and tickling all those who passed by. When they got bored with this, Kadian and Sam became nurses in the 'operating theatre', helping with the amputations, calling out for more equipment – Scissors! Scalpel! Stat! – and generally adding to the rumpus.

We had over five hundred shrieking and laughing visitors. Two children fled after getting only halfway. One girl even peed herself. We agreed that it had been a great success.

'Let's do it again next year!' said Kadian.

'I don't know,' I said. 'It was an awful lot of work.'

'Oh, Dad,' Kadian and Sam both cried, 'please, please can we do it again?'

'Fine,' I gave in. 'But only every other year, to keep it special.'

And so it was decided.

*

We agree that we should wait a few days before the burial. After all, there is a lot to do and, given our collective state of mind, we will need a little extra time to do it right. And we will need to reword the Facebook invitation.

In our enthusiasm to honour Kadian in the fullest way we had announced the burial service on Facebook, inviting all to attend. We now realised that this was a mistake, that the wooded burial site would not be able to host hundreds of people, the service would lose its intimacy, its magic. People would just have to be uninvited.

'They'll understand,' someone offers. 'Just say you've been overwhelmed by the response and now realise that the event will need to be restricted.'

The day before the service, Deb and I drive up to the burial site with James and Sam. We want to see what it looks like before we bury Kadian. Walking past the small campsite that is situated just above the burial area, Sam notes that it contains a number of tepees and yurts, a few fire pits and plenty of grass to mess around in. 'It's nice that this is not just a graveyard,' she says. 'Stuff actually happens here. Maybe we could camp ourselves.'

As we head down the dusty path through the woods I wonder how many times I will make this walk, and what my feelings will be – will it feel like coming home, or a duty that I want to shirk?

There are two young men working on the site when we arrive, holding shovels, wearing long-sleeved flannel shirts, chalk-smeared trousers and hiking boots. They are the gravediggers.

Deb explains that we are the parents of the boy who will be buried here the next day. I am surprised by the men's lack of awkwardness; they retain an open, warm demeanour, clearly used to death and the people whose lives have been shattered. It is as though they have met Kadian, that they knew him. It feels good.

I look at the hole they have been digging; it is around six feet long and six feet deep – the expression 'six feet under' chimes in my head – the hole's two parallel edges curve at both ends like a deep bathtub. What startles me is its colour. The first foot comprises black crumbling soil, but the remainder of the drop is creamy white from the downland chalk. I am relieved that I will not be dropping my son into a dark, colourless tomb, and that this will be like a coming home after all.

Kadian had a connection to chalk. At nursery school he learned to write using a stick of white chalk on a small, hand-held blackboard. Behind Bag End, our house in Oxfordshire, he played amid the crumbling white cliffs of an abandoned chalk pit. Later he carried lumps home and was thrilled when he could use them to draw shapes on the flagstones in the garden. In Shepherdstown, Kadian and Sam used to spend summer days drawing giant animal pictures on the pavement in pink, yellow and green chalk. At school, he was fascinated to learn that the chalklands had once formed the bed of some ancient sea, the chalk itself the remnants of tiny sea creatures, compressed over millennia.

As a family we regularly walked along the hills of southern England in search of giant chalk figures, visiting the white horses at Uffington, Westbury and Alton Barnes. Kadian was amazed at how the features looked so rough and unrecognisable close up, and so crisp and neatly formed at a distance. He had hiked sections of the ancient Ridgeway, the chalky path that runs from Ivinghoe Beacon in Buckinghamshire in the east to the Avebury stone circle in the west. He had clambered around the tumuli, formed of chalk and grass, where ancient chiefs had been entombed, and skipped around rings of Neolithic stones which had been upended into the chalky turf.

For Kadian chalk meant adventure, freedom, leisure and, most of all, family.

'Hampshire diamonds, that's what they call it,' says one of the gravediggers following my eyes to the chalk surrounding the grave. 'Hampshire diamonds.'

*

I had saved him before. When he was little. On the river.

It had rained for two weeks and the river was running ten foot high. I should have known better.

I was always very careful when we went canoeing. We had travelled along this stretch scores of times. I knew each bend, each hole. We all wore life vests. I knew to check the weather. To bring plenty of food and water. There was one adult for every two children on the trip. I even scouted the final section of our route to make sure we would be able to take our boats out.

But I should have known better.

Having packed the boats into the pickup truck, we left Shepherdstown and proceeded up Route 65 towards Hagerstown. Along the way we picked up two polystyrene boxes filled with freshly fried chicken thighs, packets of crinkle-cut potato chips and a few bottles of water – supplies for our trip down the creek.

We had two canoes. Kadian would be with me and Charlie in one, while Dominic and two of his kids would be in the other. Both were open-topped and painted red, both battle-worn from many a float downstream. We put in by the old stone bridge at the Devil's Backbone park. The water was running so much faster and higher than usual. The first set of rapids were nowhere to be seen. The rocks that we had so often navigated around submerged.

In the calm willow-tree-lined pool beyond we glided idly for a few minutes. We had learned long ago that to avoid the risk of losing our food downriver, when our canoes might overturn or a bag fall overboard, it was best to eat the most precious supplies early on, in the tranquil ease of this first pool. We took our time, eating, chatting, spotting wildlife – a blue heron, a pack of turtles sunning themselves on a log, a copperhead essing across the water.

And then the creek narrowed and the water picked up speed. The food and drink were stowed in a cooler tied to the canoe, paddles were withdrawn and rhythmically slotted down, back and up, and the adventure began.

We moved fast, faster than normal, unslowed by shallow waters, no need to carefully pick our way around holes or troughs or eddies. We quickly passed Butterfly Island, our usual rest spot. Today we had got here too early, so we didn't stop. Next we passed the rope swing, but the current was moving too rapidly to be able to play. Then Tornado Alley. It was here, a few years back, that many of the trees had been toppled by a tornado. The way had long since been cleared, but the name, at least to our family, had remained.

The creek narrowed once again. Our boat was in front, and I saw that our route was blocked by two trees. Branches still dripping with leaves closed the door to our way downstream. There was almost no time to react. 'Pull left,' I shouted, hoping that we could squeeze between the tip of the tree and the bank – perhaps there was enough space. Our boat turned, now perpendicular to the force of the current, and we were pushed against the tree, the weight of thousands of tons of water forcing the edge of the canoe down and propelling Kadian into the tumult. He disappeared, caught under the branches. Panic gripped my brain. No! I reached down and felt something soft, his life jacket perhaps, and yanked hard, up. Kadian followed, spluttering and crying. Charlie helped me pull him into the boat, which was leaning dangerously to one side, water pouring in – it would capsize if we didn't do something fast. 'Pull hard towards the bank,' I yelled, the noise of the water sounding louder than ever. Somehow we scraped through the gap and into the waters beyond the downed trees. Kadian was shivering and breathing hard. 'Thank you,' he said. I held him fast to my chest. I had nearly lost him. What an idiot I am, I thought to myself. Over a trip down a creek, what a stupid mistake. But instead of being furious, he had thanked me.

We were able to pull out after the last rapid, and soon we were home, taking showers, warming up, drinking hot chocolate and laughing about the adventure. But none of us forgot, least of all Kadian and me. Or Debora, who was quickly told.

I made other bad decisions. Like the time Charlie and I tried to kayak our way across a bay off the South Carolina Coast, lost our way and ended up returning against the tide in the dark, without food, water, torches or phones, and had to be rescued by the coastguard. Or another time, on the Shenandoah River, when the water ran fast and Debora and Kadian tumbled into a class III rapid, and washing-machined their way to the calmer water below, spluttering and cursing me for my earlier optimism. But none of these compared to that day, when all of us knew that we had narrowly averted disaster.

Should this have been enough of a warning? A sign that we should have bundled him up, cocooned him in bubble wrap, forbade any activity that entailed risk or danger? I don't believe that we could have succeeded, even if we'd tried.

*

One night Sam and I stay up late with friends and talk about subjects that are normally off limits. Why do bad things happen? How much do we control the world we live in?

In quiet tones we discuss the existence of God. How can He be good if He allows terrible things to occur? And if He is not good how can He exist? If God is not the beneficent grey-bearded man hovering in the heavens, the supreme being to whom we pray that everything is going to be all right, but something more ethereal, an energy, a life force lurking behind all that we see and feel, and if Kadian embodied this pure life energy, as surely he did, then where has God gone?

We talk about life after death. We all still feel Kadian in our hearts, but this is so different from having him sit across the table, taking part in the conversation, making us laugh with one of his silly jokes.

My mood darkens. I feel overwhelmed by self-pity. 'I can't believe this is happening to us,' I say. 'Why is this happening to us?'

It is late. I drink more whisky. I ask myself the questions I know we are not meant to ask. Why Kadian? Why so young? Why didn't I do more to prevent it from happening?

At one point I become disturbed by the conversation, defensive. When one of my friends suggests that she feels Kadian's presence around us, I get angry. 'Don't you realise that he's gone!' I shout. And then softer, pleading, 'I know it's hard, but we have to feel the loss. Otherwise we are deluding ourselves, we'll make things worse.'

Yet she is right. One of the confusing things about his death is that Kadian is gone, but not gone. While I know that he is not alive, that he is no longer physically present, I still feel him around, close.

Later, as I lie in bed awake, I think about this a little more. When he was alive the many strands of our relationship were indistinguishable: the feelings in my heart, my memories, our everyday interactions – chats, emails, phone calls, notes, our physical contact, his possessions, his looks, his smell.

It is only through his death that these parts separated, that I became aware of their separateness. Death, like a prism, has divided the white light of our relationship into its many colours.

But something else has happened. Since he died, some of the colours have disappeared. I have lost the violet of seeing him, the indigo of touching him, the blue of talking to him and the green of smelling him. But I can still see some of his colours. I still have the red of the feelings in my heart, the orange of his possessions, and the yellow of our memories.

Which is why it feels so confusing. He is gone, but not entirely. The white light is no longer with me, but a few of his colours remain; vibrant, illuminating. Sometimes I lose sight of even these colours. I search in the shadows, hungry for another glimpse, desperate that I may have lost them forever. Ths is my darkness.

*

Another memory blooms. I have tried to ignore this, but it is persistent. Even now I am protective of him, and I want to stop him from being hurt, again. But it says so much about Kadian, his sense of himself, his grasp of injustice.

We were living in the Old Firehall in Shepherdstown. Kadian was eleven years old. Each day, he and Sam travelled an hour on the yellow school bus to Powhatan, their school in Virginia. It was a long way but worth it; the teachers were inspiring, the facilities expansive, both kids were thriving in the rich pedagogical environment. Until now.

For a week Kadian had been coming home weary and hollow-eyed. Gone was his usual playful self. He went to bed early, his eyes were puffy. Finally we were able to coax from him what had been going on.

One day, Kadian heard a boy speak badly of another student, and then, in a disparaging way, call him 'gay'. Stepping into the conversation, Kadian challenged the boy. By this time he knew many gay people, including his piano teacher, his former nanny and the man who sold apples at the farmers' market. 'There's nothing wrong with being gay,' he said. The boy turned to Kadian and cried, 'Oh, so you must be gay as well!'

From that point on, Kadian was frequently teased for being gay. We offered to intervene, but he said he had it under control. Then, a few days later, some of the boys decided to pick on Kadian in the school changing rooms.

Distraught, Kadian ran out onto the playing field. Fearing reprisals from other students, he wasn't sure how to proceed. After some thought, he decided he must tell a member of staff. The boys were punished, and the ringleader of the group was suspended.

The next few weeks were rough. Many of the students said that they thought Kadian had exaggerated events, that the bullies had been treated harshly. Even more hurtfully, one of Kadian's closest friends at school said that she didn't believe his story and stopped talking to him.

When we heard what had happened, we offered Kadian the chance to take a few days off, but he said that would only make things worse. He wanted to stand up to the bullies. More than that, he had done nothing wrong, he said. Why should he be the one to miss classes and be forced to catch up later?

Eventually things settled down. Among some of the students, and many of the teachers, Kadian had won respect for his refusal to be intimidated.

At the end of the school year one of the bullies was told that he would not be able to return the following term. Meanwhile, Kadian had made new friends, and was busy enjoying himself.

This then is the memory. A boy who took on a bully, who

stood up for others, and made things better for everyone around him. It was all so very Kadian.

And it is this lost promise that hurts the most. How can I say it other than this? Yes we lost a son, which is unimaginable, the worst thing that can happen to a parent. But the world lost Kadian. He was going to do something extraordinary. We weren't sure what, or how. But that he would make a major contribution, of this we were certain.

*

3 August 2012

Kadian's burial. There is so much of this day that I know will be impossible. The first question is what to wear? Should it be formal, a mark of respect for the occasion, or casual and colourful, a reflection of our son?

I put on a pair of black jeans, a black T-shirt and my worn brown Blundstone work boots, just like the pair I had bought for Kadian. I wonder if I am wearing too much black, but then realise that this was what I wore most days. If people are going to judge me for it, so be it.

Deb has difficulty as well. In the end she opts for black cycling leggings, a burgundy cycling top and a neon-yellow cycling jacket. She will wear this on the bike ride to the burial service and then, if she feels like it, will change into more formal attire.

By the time we are gathered outside with our bikes – Sam and I will be riding a tandem, Deb and Charlie have a road bike apiece – everyone else has left. There is much to prepare.

Sam looks terrified. She hasn't been on a bicycle since Kadian died. None of us have. What must this do for her confidence, I think to myself, that her brother, who cycled hundreds of miles by himself, died because his brakes failed? I promise her that we will take it easy, and to call out if she feels uncomfortable at any point, and we will stop.

Before straddling the tandem, I check the brakes. They are soft. My stomach drops. There is no way I am cycling on a bike with bad brakes. I ask Charlie to take a look and after a few minutes he has them working. He has owned and managed a bicycle shop for over twenty-five years. There is nobody I would trust more.

With a wobble, we set off, a funeral cortège of terrified cyclists. I am not sure how smart this is, pedalling along country roads with diminished strength, diminished mental acuity, but it feels right, to be cycling to Kadian's burial service.

*

Kadian loved to act. He loved dressing up. He loved to be centre stage.

From a very young age he took part in performances. Aged seven, he was playing ten piano pieces at a public recital. He sang choral music in the school choir. His rock band played Coldplay's song 'The Scientist' at a pub's open mike. By the time he was thirteen his résumé read like the inside of a playbill, with leading roles in *Seussical the Musical*, *The Pirates of Penzance*, *Godspell*, *Little Red Riding Hood*, *Anne of Green Gables* and *Cinderella*.

But it was in *Snow White,* in which he was Prince Charming, that he had his standout moment. Dressed in white blouse, red velvet waistcoat, gold pantaloons, and riding a stuffed yellow-maned horse, he galloped around the stage pulling the audience's eye. When it came to his line, he paused, looked away, swished his thick brown hair out of his hazel eyes, and declared: 'It is I, Prince Charming!' The audience howled with laughter.

For months after, Kadian shone his Prince Charming smile and, with a quick turn of the head, swished his hair back. The fact is Kadian was Prince Charming, and often stole the limelight of any room he entered.

*

Kadian's basket is lying on the floor of the shelter when we arrive for the burial service. He is surrounded by sixty people, our friends and family, ready to participate in whatever type of event we have chosen for the occasion.

While we had decided that we wanted to bury him at the Sustainability Centre on the South Downs, what was less obvious to us was how the event would proceed. Should it be a memorial service or a burial? Celebratory or mournful? Who should come? In the end we had decided that we wanted three parts to the event: a sharing of memories, in which people would be invited to tell stories about Kadian, the transfer of the body to the gravesite and the burial, and then a celebration of some kind.

Deb, Sam and I sit on a bench next to Kadian's basket. To say that I am out of my comfort zone would be an understatement. My son's body is lying a couple of steps away, the same body I have cherished and protected for fourteen years, and there is nothing I can do. People come up to me and say hello, give me a hug, squeeze my shoulders. I just want the damn service to get rolling.

What does one say at such a time? I can see the anxiety on people's faces. Will they say the right thing? Can they bring us comfort? Can they bring themselves comfort?

My cousin James walks to the front of the group and introduces himself. We would be sharing stories, he says, and here is his. Whenever he came to visit us, he says – his voice falters, he smiles, then continues – he would come through the door and before he could even say hello Kadian would run towards him, jump onto him, his legs folded around his back, holding on like a koala bear, giving him a long, tight hug. It was always like this, he said, Kadian's thirst for life.

When James has finished, others take their turn. My sister Kate speaks of how great Kadian has been at playing with her young son, Nic. My friend Rupert remembers the summer when his family visited us in West Virginia, playing in the river, eating ice cream, tasting the idyllic life we had created for ourselves. My father utters a few words. I cannot remember what he says, all I see is an old man, deeply shaken by life's wicked twist.

Then it is Rob's turn. He had been Kadian and Sam's nanny when they were small. He reads out a poem that he has written for Kadian:

Magical people, it's fair to say
are very rarely found these days
You'll know when you've found one, right from the start,
It's how they see YOU, it's the size of their heart.

They know stuff that you don't, they're smart
They triumph at music and drama and art
A passion for colour, they love being loud
A magical person stands out from the crowd
Often goofy, eccentric, their humour alarming
Impeccable manners, they're beauty disarming,
In tune with nature, they're often inclined
To talk to the animals or become one at times
They love to play games, they'll hide while you seek.
They're a master of play, it's what makes them unique
They don't need approval, won't follow like sheep
Old souls, they say, leave deep prints with their feet
Magical people, it's fair to say
Teach us this lesson in their own unique way
It's not what you do that's such a big deal
What matters is how you make people feel
What we must remember, no matter what you believe
Is magical people don't really leave.

Then Deb takes a turn.

She sits down at a keyboard and plays Kadian's song. She has composed a melody for both children, each distinct, reflecting the child's personality and temperament. The piece lasts about five minutes. I think to myself, my God, she is brave and truly beautiful. What a gift to a child to know that your mother has written a song for you.

She then reads from a journal she has kept since Kadian was an infant; she has a similar book for Sam.

'So lately it has been questions about what is real. We were at Sandy's party on Sunday and you explained to Bill, her father, what a frumious bandersnatch was. "They walk like this," you said, with a limp and roll. "But they aren't real", you emphasised. So you were definitely on to it when they talked about the flying reindeer. I couldn't do it. I was afraid if I said yes, it was real, then you wouldn't trust me again. The clincher was you sat and thought, and then said, "So my stuffed animals aren't real?"'

And this.

'In your violin lesson last week you were asked if you felt it difficult to hold your violin. You said, "In my head, no – but let me ask my stomach and heart," and you lifted your shirt and spoke to your stomach and won the admiration of both your father and your teacher.'

And this.

'I tell you that children need to sleep alone so that they can grow strong and give their brains lots of space. You agree it's good to grow strong but demonstrate there is plenty of space for your brain in your bed by rolling over to the other side. I give you a big cuddle and sprinkle magic pixie fairy dust (you are very concerned about its colour and substance – it's gold glitter and like water, I tell you). I cuddle you close again and tell you that feeling stays with us in our hearts even though we sleep in separate beds. So half an hour later I hear you zipping down your slide. I come in and you have your duvet on the floor. "This way I can be closer to your heart," you say.'

There is total silence, and as she speaks, these most precious of memories hang in the air, like pixie dust. The only sound is that of gentle crying.

And then Sam stands. She tells the story of our last walk with Kadian. Two weeks before his death, the three of us had walked for eight hours through mud and non-stop rain from our house, north, across three ridges of the Hangers Way, to the small town of Alton. It had been a truly epic hike. She remembers him splashing the two of us in the puddles just before village of Selborne. She remembers him buying sweets for all three of us and then immediately eating his while we hoarded ours – later he cheekily revealed that he had stockpiled a packet of chocolate biscuits in his backpack. She remembers the joy of reaching our goal, tired but filled with a sense of achievement. She speaks confidently to the crowd, at thirteen, strong in her love for her brother, revealing her deep loss, smiling through her pain. I have never been more proud of her.

When she has finished, I speak of our last day together. What a wonderful magical day it was. The morning he had spent at the Marlborough Summer School, messing around in the swamp. Lunch with his grandparents and cousins at home. Taking his friend to town where he could buy her sweets and ice cream. And then the bike ride with his father on the Downs in the summer evening's dwindling light. Kadian saying that the countryside is so beautiful.

I mention that he had taken his bike to a shop to have the brakes fixed that very day. I want everyone to know the truth, that this was an experienced cyclist, someone who knew the roads and the footpaths of Wiltshire.

When we are done, with Kadian's beauty and charm glowing all around us, our friends and family are separated into small groups and positioned along the path that leads through the woods to the burial site. Debora, Sam and I stay behind with the eight men closest to Kadian. We stand around the basket, holding hands, silent for a few moments. Then, upon a signal from Al, the eight guardians gently carry the burial basket onto a Victorian bier, a hand-drawn wooden cart that is waiting just outside the shelter. Once secure, they take the bier's arms, and we make our way down the narrow sun-baked path, the large wheels of the bier bumping along the ruts and stones that glow pink and red from rose petals that our friends scattered earlier that morning. After a few hundred yards we come across the first group. The bier's motion is stopped. The guardians exchange places with those waiting. Then we are off again, the three of us waking just behind the bier.

Our progress is slow, methodical, the churn and creak of the wheels drumming our pace. No dream has ever felt more real. I feel as though I am floating through some Arthurian legend, the woods, the bier, the flowers, the burial basket. It is all so poignant, and so painful. As we pass the moss-covered beech trees I press my right palm against the green wet bark, marking our passage, crashing the dream to remind myself of touch and sense, while my spirit screams unreal.

After fifteen minutes or so, we arrive at his site. It has been cleaned since our last visit. The pile of chalk is now covered with a camouflage-patterned tarpaulin, the small tree that had to be cut down has been removed. The eight guardians step forward and, under Al's careful guidance, lift the basket from the bier and, with long canvas straps gliding through their hands, lower it into the chalky abyss.

Once the task has been completed, and the group has settled, someone presses play on a portable speaker system which has been brought down with us, and the opening bars of Beethoven's 9th Symphony pour into the woodland air. We had discussed this part of the service at length, baulking at the idea of further words being spoken – what else was there to say? What could be whispered as Kadian was lowered into the ground? Anything spoken would have sounded absurd or disrespectful, or both. This same music had played when Deb was in labour, when she had been desperately trying to push Kadian out of her exhausted body. It felt right to play it again, at the end, this piece so powerful, so majestic, so full of the colours of life. We worried a little that it might be too long, would people begin to fidget after five minutes, ten? In the end we agreed to play the final fifteen minutes and risk it. Another permission we gave ourselves.

Deb collapses to a half-sitting, half-kneeling position at the head of the grave. In her cycle leggings and neon jacket, a mother who has just lost her son, lamenting, weeping, moaning. All decorum is gone, there is no pretence, if there ever was, that this is a conventional, controlled display of grief. No, this is a fucking disaster and the pain is unendurable. My father leans over and tries to comfort Deb; she shrugs him off, physical touch anathema. He backs away, quickly getting the message.

I sit down next to Deb, close but not touching, Sam as well. Above, the sky has cleared and a patch of blue can be seen through the treetops. I lean back on my arms and look up, letting the music carry me away. Everyone else stands around us, not speaking, unmoving, a sign of respect for our elevated grief, shielding, holding, but not smothering, for as the music pulses and roars, we are allowed to be whatever we want, mad, strange, loud, wailing, it does not matter, as if they are saying, of course you are crazy, your son is being buried, right now, in front of us, have at it. This permission is a gift. The group feels as one, the grief so deep it is archetypal.

After the music has stopped, and a few moments have passed,

we stand. On the ground is a wicker basket of leaves taken from our garden. I take a sample and scatter them into Kadian's grave. Then, taking Deb's and Sam's hands, I set off up the path.

We are now three.

*

As we make our way back up the hill, I see the two gravediggers leaning against a fence a short, discreet distance away. As soon as the last mourner has stepped away, they will fill in the hole. The law, Al has told us, states that only one grave can be open at any one time at the burial site. They won't be able to conduct the next burial until Kadian's grave is properly filled.

Back at the lodge people drink tea and eat vegetarian food prepared from the Sustainability Centre's kitchen. I am drained. Someone brings me a piece of cake and a cup of tea. I thank them. People tell me the service was beautiful, and very moving. I had dreaded the burial part, but they were right, it was beautiful.

Then there is music.

Sitting on two stools, guitars in hand, Sam and Dominic play 'Beautiful Boy'. They have spent the last few nights working on the lyrics and the melody. Again I look on Sam with great pride. She is not someone who seeks attention but when things matter, and this does, she will step up and meet the challenge.

The song's first few verses go like this:

Right from the start
You had had an open heart
You had something special
Like you had fallen from the sky

You went on sprouting up
You couldn't laugh enough
You went places others couldn't find

Hello mate
Koala bear
Don't worry about me
I will be with you everywhere

Whoa, beautiful boy
You shared your laughter
Smiles and joy
Whoa, beautiful boy
Whoa, beautiful boy

After Sam and Dominic have finished, others follow. Philip plays a song on his guitar that he's written. Farzad has the children beating crazy rhythms on a set of bongo drums. It is chaotic, out of sync, youthful, loud and entirely appropriate.

And then it is over. It is time to go home. I can see the exhaustion I feel reflected in Sam's and Deb's eyes.

There is no way we are cycling now. Someone promises to get our bikes home safely. Someone else drives Deb and me back. Sam goes along to a pub nearby. She finds comfort in the company of others – this way she doesn't have to think too much.

Once home, Deb and I crawl into bed, hoping that when we wake up, it won't hurt as much.

*

Finn was one of Kadian's best friends from the Powhatan School. A tall, thin, gawky-looking kid, with spindly arms and braces on his teeth, Finn was sweet, smart and kind, and he liked to make movies.

One Saturday, Kadian asked if I could drive him over to Finn's house, in nearby Harpers Ferry, for a sleepover. Harpers Ferry was the charming little town where we had once camped, nestled beneath the Blue Ridge Mountains at the convergence of two of America's great rivers, the Potomac and Shenandoah. We called this spot 'almost heaven' after John Denver's song 'Country Roads': 'Almost heaven, West Virginia, Blue Ridge Mountains, Shenandoah River . . .'

Harpers Ferry was also home to the family's Cussing Bridge. In America, cussing and swearing by children is frowned upon, especially in such rural retreats as West Virginia. Growing up, our kids were constantly reminded not to cuss. Even the less extreme words, which children in England utter without recourse or complaint, are heavily frowned upon. Which is why I decided to allow the kids a brief opportunity to cuss as much as they liked.

So it was, as we reached Harpers Ferry bridge, and crossed from asphalt on land to asphalt suspended over water, the kids – Sam was in the car as well – began screaming obscenities: 'fuck, shit, bollocks' (they have an English father after all),

'fucking, fucking, fucking, fucking, turd, shit, bugger, crap, fuck!' It was both shocking and hilarious, perhaps the funniest thing I have ever heard. I realised that they knew the words, may even have spoken them to their friends, or quietly to each other, exploring the shape and sounds of these forbidden fruits, but to hear them shouted out loud, in glorious stereo, a cacophony of filth, made me tear up in joy. Sam was the quickest and the loudest; aware that the bridge would soon end, she wanted to expunge the maximum number of words she could, but Kadian was close behind, bellowing out a long stream of expletives and dirty phrases that would have earned him severe punishment, detention at least, at school. And then we were off the bridge with a rumble and they stopped, their scatological thirst quenched, at least for now.

We were still giggling as we arrived. 'See you in a couple of days,' Kadian called as he stepped out of the car towards the pretty little home, an old wooden-framed house covered with yellow-painted German clapboard and white trim.

Two days later I collected Kadian from his friend. Once we were home, he showed me what they'd been up to. He opened his laptop and clicked to YouTube. 'We have our own channel, Blue Jacket Productions,' he said. 'We've been very busy.' And they had. He showed me the films they had scripted, shot, edited and captioned in the past forty-eight hours. There was a short video of the two of them walking around the snow-covered Harpers Ferry, climbing up stairs, jumping off walls, wiping Oreo cookies across their cheeks, tearing up a piece of paper and eating it, all of which had been processed through the 'backwards' video effect. Another had Finn's mother looking for them as they appeared and disappeared in the house, this time using the blue-screen effect. But the most interesting video was one of their

longest: Finn dies, Kadian is upset at the loss of his friend, Finn's ghost tells him to look for him, Kadian goes back in time searching for him, and is finally able to bring him back to life.

This last video was about death, the sense of loss, the urge to bring the dead back to life. They were only eleven, but they understood the basics. And I wonder now, what did death mean to Kadian? How about loss and grief? It is easy to think that he had a premonition of some kind, but such thoughts make me angry. Of course he didn't – how could he? Whenever my mind drifts into such territory I give myself a mental slap. Such teleological thinking is comforting, for sure, there lies its attraction, but I fear where it will take me. For if Kadian knew of his impending death, why didn't he do something about it? Is he somehow to blame for it? Perhaps he sought it. Of course, such thinking is nonsense, which is why I refuse to go there. These were just two kids playing around with ideas that they are surrounded by. Death and dying are everywhere, sanitised for the most part for children, but still around, in movies and television shows, books and newspapers. And yet my mind searches for hidden meanings; it constantly tries to make sense of what happened, where I fear there is none.

'This is the best one,' Kadian told me as he clicked on another YouTube thumbnail, 'We call it the "Liver Song".'

Kadian was a funny boy. He was funny in the conventional sense, learning jokes from books and then retelling them to family members. He created sentences that punned with double meanings, and arranged elaborate pranks for his sister and friends – these often involved water balloons. But he was also funny in a different, off-the-wall, unique way. For weeks he would insert the same non sequitur word into sentences, and the effect was both bizarre and amusing. He started adding an

extra 'gurt' to the end of people's names, as in Milo-gurt, Sam-gurt, Finn-gurt. He made up silly songs, one of which, 'The Birthday Cake Song', was so popular, that he recorded it onto CDs and sold it to his friends at school.

Perhaps Kadian's most celebrated comic moment, posted on Facebook and enjoyed by many, was his performance of the Parrot Sketch for the school's talent show. Teaming up with his friend Nathan, he memorised the entire script and, dressed up in his mother's long trench coat, the closest thing to the gentleman's jacket that John Cleese had worn on television, and holding a lantern, the closest thing we could find to a birdcage, in which lay a stuffed multicoloured parrot, Kadian delivered a near perfect rendition of the Monty Python classic.

'This parrot is no more!' he roared. 'He has ceased to be!' Kadian screamed in a brilliant cockney accent. ''E's expired and gone to meet 'is maker! 'E's a stiff! Bereft of life, 'e rests in peace! If you hadn't nailed 'im to the perch 'e'd be pushing up the daisies! 'E's kicked the bucket, 'e's shuffled off 'is mortal coil, run down the curtain and joined the bleedin' choir invisible! He's snuffed it!' Then pulling the parrot out of the 'cage', Kadian smashed the stuffed animal three times against the table, held it up for examination, demonstrating its lack of movement and declared: 'THIS IS AN EX-PARROT!'

But the 'Liver Song', filmed with Finn that weekend, is my favourite. In it, Kadian appears amid the pile of large grey boulders that made up Jefferson's Rock in Harpers Ferry. He magically disappears and reappears from one shot to another, then crawls menacingly towards the camera, singing, 'I am going to eat your liver, bawoop, bawoop, I am going to eat your liver, bawoop, bawoop, liver, liver, liver, liver.' The next scene has him loudly sucking a glass of milk through a long straw shaped

like a pair of spectacles, saying, 'The liver is really delicious, yeehaw!' The video ends with a close-up of him lying on a giant colour photograph of a gory liver, his mouth open as if he wants to eat it, the song continuing in the background. It was totally silly, very funny, full of his zest and zeal for life.

Where is that zest and zeal now?

PART III

Kadian loved to tease.

He teased me about my cooking. 'Have you ever cooked before?' he would ask when I presented him with some burnt or underdone concoction I'd painstakingly prepared. He liked to tease me about my driving. 'You are ten miles over the speed limit, Dad.' And he liked to tease me about my telephone skills. 'Dad, you won't get anywhere if you're rude to the customer service reps.'

Most of all he liked to tease me about my hair.

My hair had started thinning in my early thirties. At first, I didn't think it was anything to worry about. All the men in our family had receding hairlines, or 'high foreheads', as we liked to call it. Deb didn't notice, or if she did, she didn't comment on it. But sometime in my early forties, when Kadian was around eleven, he started calling it to my, and then, soon after, everyone else's attention.

'Do you want to know their names?' he would ask total strangers. 'This one,' he said, pointing to a small patch of hairlessness at the top of my head, 'is called Larry.' The person would laugh, inevitably. 'This one,' he would say, moving his fingers lower, 'is called Mary. Mary is married to Larry.' More chuckles. 'And this one,' he was now near back of my head, 'is Jerry, their son.'

The truth, and I only acknowledged this when I was alone, looking in the mirror, was that I was rapidly going bald. Not an acceptable, all-over, symmetrical crescent-shape baldness, this was more like mange: spotty and random.

The best solution was to shave the whole thing off. Which I did, one morning, while the kids were still asleep. It's not an easy thing, to shave one's head. It requires different movements – side-to-side, front-to-back, back-to-front, over-and-under – you need both hands, and you need a lot of soap or shaving cream. In the end I looked like a very badly shorn sheep.

Deb suggested I used some of her Nair product to obtain that shiny Mr Clean look. I applied a palmful of pinkish goop to my head, rubbed it in, rinsed my hands and went downstairs for breakfast. Job done.

The kids were shocked at first, but by that afternoon, they were excitedly showing off my sparkly scalp to anyone who cared to look. That night, as we were going to bed, I told Deb that my head was feeling rather hot. 'It's probably razor burn,' she suggested. Probably.

At around three in the morning I woke in a panic, my head on fire. What was going on? I ran to the bathroom and looked in the mirror. My scalp was bright red. This couldn't be razor burn. Fumbling around under the sink I looked for the Nair bottle. I read the directions: 'Rinse after ten minutes.' Shrieking, I ran into the shower and rinsed it off.

When I told Kadian what had happened in the morning he

roared with laughter. And for the next few days he had a great time commenting on my pink head, since now he had another thing to tease me about.

*

I have started reading *A Grief Observed*, C. S. Lewis's account of his wife's death, and of his life after it. I had seen *Shadowlands*, the film based on it, and remember sobbing – when they visit their secret valley together, when he says his last words to her, his loneliness. But I did not know death then. Lewis wrote that the book was based on four notebooks he filled with thoughts and poems after his wife's death. I decide I need to start writing.

But when I pick up my pen, I find I that I can't. This surprises me. Writing is all I have done lately – my book on my Nazi-hunting uncle has been recently acquired by a publisher. In fact, I need to start editing it soon. But I don't have the energy, the focus or the willpower.

I try something else. I haven't written poetry for years. I started when I was thirteen as I travelled with my grandmother around England and Scotland. Somewhere, on the banks of a loch, near Ullapool, I sat on a rock and wrote a few lines on a scrap of paper. And I was hooked. My writing turned darker during my teenage years; inspired by Sylvia Plath and Seamus Heaney, I wrote about Jewish jackboots and the dead who speak from their graves. Then, in my twenties, now occupied with the outside world – girls, work, politics, friends – I stopped.

I open a notebook and write without thinking:

I feel like I'm a tuning fork
Vibrating after someone has hit me
And I can't stop shaking

I am surprised to be writing. I can't make myself lunch, but my hand appears able to form words on a page. I try again:

I am breaking.
Can I be strong enough to hold it together
For Sam?
Should I be strong enough?

It comes directly out of one of my brains. The animal brain. The fight-or-flight, horror-and-fear, love-and-excitement brain. Unfiltered emotion formed into inexact words.

I search for you
In the boy
Who cycles down my street
Under your covers in your room
In the faces of the pupils
Heading to class at your school
I will keep on searching

I don't read what I have written. I don't review or edit. I turn the page, and start another one:

I am not contagious
Do not cross the road
I may cry

When you see me
Do not be scared

I write ten poems, one after the other, without rest.

While he thought I was marvelling
At his new Apple product
I was marvelling at
Him, my boy, my unboxer

It is as if they are pre-formed in my head. All I have to do is write them down. It's like singing the words to a song I know.

We liked to tussle
He and I
Not Graeco with throws and falls
Nor judo with rolls and holds
With tickles and giggles on the sofa
This was love wrestling

A few days later I look at what I have written. Some of it I find startling – off-centre, disassociated, perhaps even inappropriate. But many lines make me smile. And then, in a fit of unselfconsciousness, and possibly stupidity, I post one of the poems on Facebook.

Comments are posted almost immediately. I am surprised by the responses: 'Happy beautiful memory', says a friend from America. 'This is brilliant', says one of his school friends, 'Keep them coming', says a third.

I decide to continue writing.

*

We are in the kitchen making breakfast. Sam makes her own – Nutella smeared thick on whatever bread we happen to have in the larder. I have long given up trying to limit her Nutella habit. These small fights, I just don't have the strength for them.

This was one of the first casualties of Kadian's death. If Sam wants to spend seven hours of a Sunday watching television on her computer, fine. If she wants to sleep until two in the afternoon, fine. If she doesn't want to come out with us on a walk, fine. If she refuses to accompany us to a friend's house for dinner, preferring to stay at home, feed herself ramen noodles, fine. Frankly, how can such things matter, considering?

And yet, I think to myself, they do.

Sam, a young lady with a clear sense of her own needs and capabilities, also exhibits a very unusual lack of judgement. A few weeks after Kadian's accident we usher her – only thirteen, fearful of strangers, never having been on this journey before – onto a train from Petersfield to Brighton, amid the lager-swigging foul-mouthed swearing louts who inhabit the trashed carriage, and walk away. She arrives at her destination, unscarred, but she is shaken, and surprised that she ended up on this train, a train she would usually have refused to take. It is reassuring, surprisingly, to see that our disturbance is shared by Sam. Though we are concerned enough that we ask our close friends to monitor all our decisions until further notice when it comes to Sam. With teenagehood now on the horizon, we want to ensure that we are making the right parental calls.

And this leaves me with a profound sense of discomfort and lack of confidence. Should Sam spend the night with a friend whose parents I don't know? Should she be able to visit a shop by herself? Go for a walk, watch a movie, travel by train? The list goes on. I was unaware of how many parental decisions I made each day. Now I find I default to Debora, and when she defaults back to me, we default to Sam. Not always the right move.

Which leads to my fear that Sam will become the parent, we the children. She will bury her grief, tend to us, her collapsed parents who spend their days in bed, watching television reruns, buried under the covers, unable to interact with the world, as she progresses through her schooldays, and on, to life beyond. We her millstone, to be carried for the rest of her days; because of her golden heart, she will not be able to discard it, even when it weighs her down. The guilt of this presses down on me, as if a tower block has been lowered onto my head. And even though I wake up to have breakfast with her each morning, and greet her when she returns from school, I am never fully able to get out from under the shadow of this anxiety.

*

Two weeks after Kadian's death the doorbell rings. There are two policemen standing outside, both dressed in regulation black trousers, black jackets, black shiny shoes, black caps with white stripes – perfect mourners.

We sit around our kitchen table, the policemen on one side, Debora and I on the other. We discuss whether Sam should also be present. Is it best for her to feel part of the process, or should we shield her from the details? We decide to let her sleep in.

'First let me offer my condolences,' PC Trafford says somewhat stiffly. He has put his hat on the table, his short black hair is brushed back and glistens with cream. 'As I explained over the phone, we're here to take a statement from you, and to answer any of your questions.' He describes the process to us. He is currently taking statements from the witnesses, and has commissioned a forensic expert to examine the bicycle. An inquest will open the following week. It will last for only a minute or so, long enough to declare that further information is required. It will close for a few months while the police gather that information. A longer inquest will then be held, possibly next spring. We will, at some stage, be allowed to see the police reports and witness statements.

'I have to warn you,' he says, 'that these types of cases are very hard to prosecute. The most likely charge is criminal negligence, and having already spoken to my supervisor, I can tell you that it is extremely rare to get such cases to court. The evidence threshold is steep. This doesn't mean you can't pursue a claim through the civil courts, however. There the standard of proof is lower.'

Trafford then asks if I am ready to give a statement. I say I am and suggest that we go upstairs. Some part of me feels that by showing him Kadian's room he will feel the loss more greatly. It is a vain and transparent attempt at manipulating the situation.

We sit in the two white armchairs that I had purchased for my chic real-estate office in Shepherdstown, and which Kadian had claimed for his bedroom when we moved back to England. Bicycle tools lie in a plastic box next to the green-and-white-striped sofa – which I had picked up from a dump and which still smells of old-man and cigarettes – the grease from Kadian's bicycle tyres still smears the walls by the bedroom door.

'Just start at the beginning,' Trafford says. 'Tell me what happened in the lead-up to the collision.'

Collision? It wasn't a collision. How could a bicycle being hit by a van travelling at sixty miles an hour be a collision? A collision implies two objects hitting each other at equal speed. Kadian was struck by the van, his bicycle was smashed by the van's grille, Kadian was catapulted from the grille into the van's windscreen and onto the road. The van was the perpetrator, Kadian the victim. The equivalence and neutrality of 'collision' fill me with anger.

'Kadian was hit by the van,' I say. 'It was not a collision.'

'OK, tell me about what happened before Kadian was hit by the van.'

This is the first time I have systematically gone through the events of that day. I realise that there are holes in my memory. Certain periods take up more space than others. I am not sure how much time had elapsed between one point and the next. I see some images clearly – riding down the path, laughing and calling out to each other – while others are fleeting, incomplete, shaky, like a television that is not quite tuned to the correct frequency.

*

Kadian's passion for Apple products began on his tenth birthday when he received an iPod Nano. He loved this little green tin box of musical tricks, carrying it everywhere, on the way to school, around the house. He even listened to it in the bath, despite my repeated warnings.

Two years later he told us he wanted to upgrade to an iPod Touch. The key difference, he explained, was that the Touch could access the Internet via Wi-Fi, and with this he could access the world. He could Skype his mother when she was in Washington DC. He could order pizza from Domino's. He could research the latest trends in technology. We told him it was fine with us, but he had to earn the money to pay for it.

Within a few days he had set up his own account on Amazon and sold his iPod Nano. But he was still a few hundred dollars short. So when fourteen inches of snow fell in Shepherdstown, Kadian, Sam and a friend pulled on their ski trousers and jackets, donned gloves, thick socks and boots, and, with shovels in hand, set off to assist the good citizens of the town.

After twelve hours of non-stop shovelling, they had made three hundred dollars, each. By the time he was in bed that evening Kadian had ordered his iPod Touch.

Six months later he wanted to upgrade again. Now he wanted a MacBook Pro. This was a tall order – he would need over a thousand dollars. He sold his beloved Lionel train collection on a hobbyist website and his keyboard on eBay, and even set up his own business selling books on Amazon. He shovelled more snow, saved up birthday money and took care of the neighbours' pets. And after nine months of hard work he had his beloved MacBook Pro.

He adored his Apple products, and, as he learned more about them, became a fan of the Apple Corporation itself, and in particular its founder, Steve Jobs. 'Did you know that Steve Jobs dropped out of college?' he would tell me when we were talking about possible universities he might be interested in. 'Did you know that Steve Jobs built his first computer in his father's garage?' he would say when asking to borrow one of my tools (having failed to return one that he had borrowed the day before).

He spent his free time watching YouTube videos in which

Steve Jobs presented the latest product to a packed Apple conference. He could list the names of the top Apple executives, becoming particularly fond of Jonathan Ive, the designer of some of the company's most iconic products. Kadian could describe the particular luminescence of a retina screen display, the speed of a dual core processor, the virtues of the hi-tech material used in the unibody case.

For Christmas, he asked his grandparents for a subscription to *Macworld*. He would study each issue from first page to last, absorbing the recent news of Apple products, upgrades and software, and presenting his own opinions on a blog which he had recently started.

One day, at breakfast, he placed that month's issue of *Macworld* on the table and casually mentioned that they had published his letter to the editor. Deb and I read the letter, which was titled 'Not Appy about Apps', and which launched a scathing attack on Microsoft's tendency to copy Apple innovations. 'That's so great, Kads!' I said, when I had finished reading. He smiled. Later he posted the letter on Facebook.

*

The last few seconds of Kadian's life keep flashing through my head, like a series of film frames on a continual loop: We are heading down the final slope, Kadian drifts ahead of me, away from me, I see the van speeding from left to right, Kadian is hit and dragged out of sight. The memory has the feel of a 1950s home movie; too much contrast, the sound too crisp, the colours too rich. I see it again and again and again.

Is this post-traumatic stress disorder? Am I having flashbacks? Or is this just a memory – horrific, shocking – but only a memory? Deb tells me I need help.

A week later I am sitting in front of a therapist. She has a thick Greek accent and is warm and welcoming. She offers me a glass of water. From her window I can see a wide swathe of trees swoosh back and forth in the wind. She expresses her thoughts with elaborate gesticulations. And she talks to me. There are no periods of uncomfortable silence.

I tell her that I don't know why I should continue living, that I have no urge to move forward, that my life has ended, that I am truly broken. She pauses for a moment and then tells me that it is through Sam that I will find meaning. 'Hold on to that thread,' she says. 'Hold on to that thread.'

I am grateful to be in the hands of someone who is confident, someone who will take command of my rudderless ship.

I then tell her about the looped images. She tells me that she is not surprised, that they are symptoms of PTSD, that I am likely to be experiencing both grief and shock. In fact, she says, I look as if I am still in shock. I question her – surely shock only lasts a short while, a few hours at most. I have had shock before – your knees feel week, your heart races, you feel a little unstable. No, she says, you can feel shock for weeks, even months. What I had experienced was the worst thing that anyone could experience. I had witnessed the violent death of my child.

As I leave, I pull the therapist's front door behind me, but not all the way. A sign perhaps that I need to come back.

On the way home I notice that I cannot drive more than forty miles an hour, even on major roads. Drivers flash and honk at me, but I can't bring myself to press the accelerator any harder. To do so would be to make the world flick by too fast. I hunker close to the kerb, sometimes going over the white line, wanting only to get home and climb under the bed covers.

Late into the night, around two or three in the morning, I talk to Deb again about the memory – which I have now titled 'The Final Fifteen Seconds'. The final fifteen seconds, cycling through the woods, laughing and calling to each other, the descent, Kadian pulling ahead, me not being able to reach out to him, Kadian being hit by the van. Over and over again. Each time making my body shake in terror.

She tells me that she feels a similar pain. She was stranded halfway round the world, sitting at the end of a phone as medics pounded away at her son's chest, trying to bring him back to life.

'I'm glad you were there,' she says, 'it is beautiful that you were there.'

The words make me angry. How could she be glad? How could it be beautiful?

She sees my reaction, and continues. 'If you hadn't been there it would have been worse. We would have wondered, "Did he suffer?" Because you were there we know that he did not. It is beautiful because you were there for his birth, and you were there for his death. If it was going to happen, as a parent, how else would you want it to be?'

The workings of the brain are a mystery to me, no more so than in these days after the accident. Her words are like salve to my soul. A knot in my brain has been unpicked. From this point on 'The Final Fifteen Seconds' stops its incessant cycle. She has given me a tremendous gift. Not only by transforming a moment of iconic horror into one of magic, but she has given me hope that, with a little compassion and insight, my madness might abate.

*

For years I was the owner of a BlackBerry smartphone. I worshipped it, relying on its email function and easy Internet access. It allowed me to do business on the run, keep track of my clients, it was a key weapon in my multitasking arsenal.

But Kadian teased me about it. My 'CrackBerry' was out-of-date and uncool, he said. After a year of relentless lobbying, I gave in, and purchased an iPhone. He was so happy. He swore that he would convert the entire family to Apple products by the end of 2011.

Kadian himself had recently bought an iPhone 4S, and now that I too had an Apple product, he invited me to help him make an unboxing video, comparing his mother's old iPhone 4 to his new upgraded device. I would record the video on the iPhone I had just purchased.

Sitting at his hi-tech aluminium and glass desk, Kadian prepared for the shoot. The week before he and I had painted the wall behind him metallic grey, the same colour as a MacBook Pro. On the wall was stencilled a giant white Apple Inc logo and the words 'Think Different'. Above him on a wide shelf stood an array of white Apple boxes that he had collected over the years: iMac, iPad, MacBook Air, MacBook Pro, iPhone 4, iPhone 4s, iPod Touch and iPod Nano. It was an altar to the Apple gods.

I pressed record and he started talking. He was fluent, charismatic, engaging, interesting. He compared the two phones in front of him, pointing out their similarities and differences. Peeling the plastic cover off the new phone, he turned it on, allowing the viewer a moment to wonder at its craft and beauty, and quickly explaining the exciting new features that the phone boasted.

Through my viewfinder I looked on, impressed. He was a natural storyteller, having mastered the skills of arc and pace. Though the subject matter appeared, at least to me, to be inherently boring, his manner captivated me. How had he learned to do this? At his age I was scared to speak in the classroom, let alone speak unscripted, on a technical subject, without hesitation, for eight minutes to a public audience he has never met, and is unlikely to. The kid should be on television, I thought to myself.

*

Three weeks after Kadian died the parcels start arriving in the mail. Desperate for a road map out of our madness, Deb had ordered a pile of books from Amazon.

For as long as I have known her, Deb has sought mastery of her world through books. There was a time when we had over 10,000 tomes in our house. Books were stacked in wobbly piles on tables, counters, even on the floor. When we moved from the USA back to England we gave most of the books away, Deb promising to relocate her library to her iPad. But with Kadian's death, her need for paper-based products returned, and for this I was thankful. Like her, I needed a road map out of our new-found hell. Surely there was someone out there who could help us.

I start with the best-sellers. Most of these are based on the premise that grief is something that you recover from, that you surmount. They are prescriptive, suggesting that grief is comprised of a series of distinct stages that one must travel through, as if hurdles to jump over in a steeplechase. The most famous book is by Elisabeth Kübler-Ross, *On Grief and Grieving: Finding the Meaning of Grief Through the Five Stages of Loss*, in which she lays out five distinct stages: denial, anger, bargaining, depression and acceptance.

None of these books speak to how I feel. They confuse me. They leave me with a deep sense of unease and inner conflict. For how can grief be something that I want to recover from? The concept feels disloyal to Kadian. And if I no longer grieve his loss doesn't that mean that I don't value him, that I don't miss him? As to the 'five stages of loss', I seriously doubt that everyone experiences the same process of grief as if it were some Newtonian law. I suspect that my experience will be far messier, without neat periods of beginnings and ends.

I plough on with my marathon reading session. I am told time and again that things will 'get better', that I must be patient, that though the pain feels too much now, it will lessen. Angrily, I toss these books aside. The most offensive, I tear into sections and dump in the woodshed behind our house.

Thankfully, there are exceptions to this litany of literary self-help bullshit. Within these few I find not only wisdom, but gentle counsel. I connect with their candour, I am liberated by their brutal honesty, I am guided to calm respite.

In *The Year of Magical Thinking*, Joan Didion describes her life after her husband of forty years dies of a heart attack. 'On most surface levels I seemed rational,' she writes. But not on all levels. Didion, a woman of letters known to be sensible and even-headed, confesses that she sensed, magically, that her husband was still present in her house. Her words reassure me.

I too have, somewhat alarmingly, sensed Kadian. I speak to him in the quiet moments of the morning when I am half asleep and my internal editor has not yet clicked in. I see him in the garden mowing the lawn. I catch a glimpse of him out of the corner of my eye as I eat my cereal in the morning.

I am intrigued by Didion's style. She tells it like it is, recounting her experience with brutal honesty, sprinkling her unvarnished prose with raw facts. For instance, she describes the medical cause of her husband's death in graphic detail, as she does the unsuccessful intervention of the emergency workers. Her writing is objective, detached, clear-sighted, which appeals to me as an investigative journalist and former documentary maker. As I read her book I realise that I too have a thirst for the facts that surround Kadian's death.

I also look at Rabbi Harold Kushner's book, *When Bad Things Happen to Good People*. I read that those who have lost a loved one often feel that they deserve tragedy, that they have it coming, a result of some universal karmic force. This way of thinking can quickly lead to self-loathing, self-abuse and depression. The rabbi writes that the power of condolence is that people gather around you and say, 'This is terrible, but you don't deserve it, you are a good person.' When I read this I tremble, the knowledge confirming my own thought processes. I feel a profound sense of gratitude for all those who have gathered around us.

In Viktor Frankl's *Man's Search for Meaning*, he describes his experiences as a Jewish prisoner in Auschwitz. I am fascinated to read about his attempt to find meaning in such a hellish situation – is it really possible? Most of all, I am struck by his description of his own mental process, that even as he arrived at the camp he became acutely aware not only of the shouting of the guards, the miserable conditions and the fear tearing at the other prisoners, but also of his own curiosity, and that this impulse to learn and understand, to gain mastery of even the worst situations, provided him with some small comfort. I realise that I have been ashamed of my own curiosity; Frankl gives me permission to observe my own reactions to Kadian's death.

And I gain solace in the writings of the contemporary philosopher Ken Wilber, particularly his *Grace and Grit*, in which he describes the final few months of the life of his wife, Treya. As she lies on her deathbed, the victim of aggressive cancer, she begs him to search for her in the years to come. He reluctantly promises, 'I'll find you, honey, I will . . .' knowing that he is agreeing to the impossible. But, in the months after her death, and this is the part I find helpful, he realises that he has indeed found her. For Treya had extraordinary integrity, honesty and compassion, and every time he meets these characteristics, he knows that he has met the mind and soul of his wife.

I wonder, can this be a way forward, a way to keep Kadian close even though he is gone? Though it sounds simple on paper, in practice this feels like a stretch. How can I hold him fast if I know he is dead? Shall I hope to overcome grief, as the self-help gurus have suggested? Will the pain subside over time?

*

I have become an expert in hugs.

There are the love hugs. These are given by the people who have fully confronted the severity of the situation, allowed themselves to be vulnerable to its magnitude, who are able to be with me, unreservedly.

Then there are those who deliver the quick clasp and release, who are sympathetic, but uncomfortable, committed but disconnected. Sometimes these people, often men, pat me on the back, as if burping a baby, hoping for me to sick up my grief.

Finally, there are the non-huggers, people who never embrace, yet who are compelled to in this extreme situation. I feel relieved when they back away.

Kadian's death hasn't changed any of my relationships, it has just made them clearer. The people I already felt comfortable with, I still feel comfortable with. It doesn't matter what they do or say, only that they are here, with me. While others, whose company I have previously found awkward, can utter no words of solace, can perform no acts that will make me feel loved or secure. I have learned, and it has taken a while to discover this, a lot of heartache, that it is best to avoid these people altogether.

Such thinking may sound judgemental, ugly, even toxic. Surprisingly, and embarrassingly, a large amount of my time after the accident has been spent caught up in this type of analysis, cataloguing my behaviour as well as the behaviour of those around me. Who called to share their condolences? Who did not? Did people say 'Kadian passed away' or 'Kadian died', or resist naming the tragedy at all?

I have also become obsessed with words: the many nuances and meanings of phrases and expressions, the tone in which they are delivered. Since Kadian's death, I have become fascinated by what people say to us. I am an aficionado of grief expressions. Perhaps it is my way of taking control of a situation in which I have lost all control. The most common are stock phrases which actually pop up when you search the Internet for 'things you should say to people who are grieving'. These include: 'I am so sorry for your loss', 'my condolences', and 'if there is anything we can do . . .'

But the one that is most often repeated, the one which I hate the most, is 'There are no words . . .' This drives me nuts. There are so many words. Like 'Our world is broken', or 'How is it possible to keep living?', or 'Kadian was the most beautiful boy', or 'Why the fuck is this happening to us?'

Oddly, the same words can be uttered by different people with opposite effects: some reassure, while others offend. I can never quite figure this out.

*

Kadian first logged on to Facebook in December 2008. He posted a picture of Duke. 'He is so cute!' he wrote. He listed that he was thirteen. In fact he was ten.

He was an efficient and consistent Facebook user. He didn't linger over his posts or waste hours stalking the lives of others. To him, Facebook was a useful place to share news, pictures, interests. As a result, we have a remarkable record of his last four years.

There are many memorable postings, snapshots of his life as a growing teenager. Firing off rockets in a friend's yard. Watching his friends play air hockey. Baking cakes. Going for bike rides. Dressing up for Halloween. Pictures of his latest Apple gadget.

Often his notes were pithy. For example, he wrote: 'Kadian

is bloated after a nice donut breakfast', and then a few weeks later, 'Kadian is pumped after a three mile run', and 'Kadian + Bus + Coldplay = Good Mood.'

Others posts gave a flavour of his life. 'Woke up this morning with music blasting from downstairs. I left my door open for my cats, so Sam peaked in and said, "We're going for breakfast, wake up and get dressed." So now I'm downstairs next to the pulsating speaker facebooking, and it feels like I AM the only one awake.'

In his Facebook 'notes' section, he listed '25 random things about me' (there are 26):

1. I am completely addicted to my dog, putting up images and his name willy-nilly.
2. I fantasise about living on the Caribbean island St Lucia.
3. I have an earring in my left ear, I hugged a teddy bear when I got it pierced.
4. I spend a lot of time on my Lionel train layout.
5. My sister and I are Irish twins, I was born in 1998, she was born in 1999.
6. I love to bake, my latest masterpiece was a cake I created for my sister's tenth birthday.
6. I have an autographed Hillary Clinton sign hanging up in my bedroom, although I was an Obama supporter from the very beginning.
7. When I was born I had a stretched blue cone head and my parents called me Stodge.
8. For the first six years of my life, my parents double-barrelled me and called me Kadian Cackler-Harding.
9. I have been playing piano since I was four and take lessons from the one and only Dr Scott Beard.

10. There is a sliding brick in our wall by the staircase and me and my sister hide random bits and bobs behind it.
11. My mother is a champion pillow and blanket fort builder while I specialise in stick ones at school.
12. My sister's future career will be in the House of Sam fashion shop.
13. After my cat's fat uncle Max passed away, I gave her a cuddle every night.
14. I am a serious runner chasing after my dog while he does the same to a squirrel.
15. My father always tells me to put on more layers than I need.
16. My sister and I have a bathroom of our own, while we choose to use our parents'.
17. I have always wondered why we bathe instead of vacuum ourselves off.
18. I aggressively attack sugar while my dog aggressively attacks his stuffed ducks.
19. I had braces for four years and I now sleep with a retainer every night.
20. I studied Rome for a year and when I went to the place itself, I almost fainted.
21. I moved from a house in Oxford, to a cottage in the middle of nowhere, to an RV for six weeks, to an Old Firehall.
22. I home-schooled for three years and then went to a tiny school with only twenty-five people.
23. I did a Monty Python sketch for my school talent show.
24. Some of the things I miss most about England are chocolate, pork pies and sausages.
25. My first word was Mumma.

Kadian uploaded his last Facebook post on 20 July 2012. After a shooting at a cinema in the US he wrote: 'My heart goes out to those affected by the shootings in Colorado.'

*

In the first few days after Kadian's death, Deb goes into his room every night. When I ask her what she does in there, she says she tucks him in, runs through what has happened that day.

For my part, I go into his bedroom every morning. I open the door and turn on the lights. 'Good morning,' I say. 'Time to get up'. Then, half looking at his bed, I pull the covers back. 'It's going to be a beautiful day, Kads.'

Everything is exactly as he left it. Two empty pint glasses stand on the grey filing cabinet next to his desk. Each night he would drink one pint. Then he would soak in a long, piping-hot bath. Now over-heated, and thirsty once again, he would drink the second pint before going to bed.

Against the wall leans his bicycle stand. There are tyre marks on the wall. School books and files are strewn across the floor. A pile of computer carcasses are stacked in one corner. His backpack overspilling with bike gear sits in another.

Around week two, something changes. When I try going in I feel, and hear, a slam to my body, as if I have walked into glass. Deb says she feels the same. It is like walking into blackness, nothingness, like stepping off a cliff.

Now, every time I walk past his bedroom, I look ahead and walk straight down. But sometimes I glance to my left, and if the door is ajar, I am hit by a wave of nausea.

One month after Kadian's death people start asking us about 'cleaning up' his room. It is as if there is a collective recognition that it is time to do something. What will you do with his bedroom? What will you be keeping?

Sam is adamant that nothing should be touched. I am fairly content to leave things as they are, but Deb wants to put away the things away that trigger the worst pain – most of all she is upset about the loose strands of hair that still lie on his pillowcase.

We begin to discuss it every day. Sometimes twice a day. Deb still thinks we should tidy it up. I resist until, one day, I switch my position. I say it must be cleaned, that it's unhygienic to leave it as it is. I can't stand it. My son's room, abandoned. I am not sure if cleaning up will make a difference, but I am willing to give it a try.

The conversation turns into a question of parenting. Are we being good parents by allowing Sam the space to resist change? Would it be better to help her through it by firmly saying that the clean-up must take place? Friends tell us we need to give her sufficient time to grieve, but to set a specific date to act. We agree that we will clear the room up by Thanksgiving, in November. Sam isn't pleased but agrees, with the proviso that items in their shared bathroom – such as Kadian's stock of deodorant bottles – will not be touched.

We make it to September. Sam is preparing for her first term at Bedales, the same school that Kadian had attended. Bedales is located three hundred yards down the road in a beautiful 120-acre campus, and is justly celebrated for its liberal tradition and for its focus on excellence, no matter the subject: theatre, mathematics, music or carpentry. Our family has gone to Bedales for generations: Kadian and Sam's aunt, uncle, grandmother and great-grandfather all attended.

But now, it is all too much. Kadian's school books are still on his bedroom floor, as if he will be going back on Monday morning.

Deb cracks. She begs Sam for permission to put the books away. The rest of the room could remain as it is, but the books at least should be tidied. Sam resists. Feeling trapped, Deb bursts into tears. She wants to look out for Sam, who is anxious about starting her new school, but can't focus on her until Kadian's room is taken care of. She makes herself vulnerable, explaining her feelings, and together they walk upstairs. They reach an agreement. Deb can clear up the books, but nothing else. 'Don't move that,' Sam says, pointing at a bicycle wrench on Kadian's glass table. 'You said only the school stuff, Mum.' Deb puts down the wrench and returns to clearing up the books.

A few minutes later they are both downstairs, Deb visibly shaken. Sam withdrawn, but thankfully not too upset.

I go upstairs to check on the room. My chest tightens as I enter. Not much has changed, but there is order. His bed has been made. Books have been put away.

On the windowsill I notice a ball that I'd found earlier that year in a second-hand shop in Berlin. It was covered with multi-coloured tiles, silver beads and a few small mirrors. I'd thought Kadian would like it, and it was cheap. When I gave it to him he looked intrigued. 'Thanks, Dad,' he had said politely, turning it over in his hand, and then putting it to one side. But he hadn't thrown it away or hidden it, he'd kept it.

*

Another memory from my teenage years cuts into view. I was on a year-long bicycle ride from Bolivia to the USA and had got as far as Toledo, a small town outside Mexico City.

I had spent the afternoon at a rodeo with my three cycling companions, but had become bored, and cycled on ahead. Seeing some children playing with a large tyre, I stopped, wheeled my bicycle onto the side of the road, and took out my camera to take some photographs. When I came to I was in the back of a car. 'You've had an accident,' said my friend Alex. 'You were hit by a van. Luckily the accident happened outside a doctor's house. He's driving us to hospital.'

The next thing I remember was lying on a hard surface, perhaps in an operating room. I heard a man giving my friend Meryl a list of things to purchase: 'Bandages, anaesthetic, needles, thread,' I heard him say, 'You can find it all at the old lady's shop around the corner.' Meryl was back a short while later and I felt a sharp object being pushed through my scalp. I ended up with twenty-five stitches in my head.

That night, when I woke up, it was very dark. I was disorientated and woozy, a combination of the drugs they'd put me on, and my body's own response to the pain. I climbed out of bed, groped my way to the door of my room, and then out into a narrow corridor. Shuffling forward, I felt the walls on either side. Ahead of me was a door with a small portal window. I saw light on the other side, and walked towards it. I pushed through the door and saw two men dressed in green medical aprons standing next to a body. They were performing an autopsy. 'You shouldn't be here,' said one of the men in Spanish. I nodded, apologised, turned and left.

This episode has stuck with me for years. It has the feel of a memory rather than a dream, but it is so strange, so disturbing. A teenager, injured in a cycling accident, walking into an autopsy, which perhaps should have been his.

I am on the phone to the police – one of our many conversations in those first few days after Kadian's accident. I ask them if Kadian had an autopsy. They say yes. It had taken place in the Swindon hospital. It must have been after we had seen him but before he was transported back to Hampshire. I express surprise, but the policeman says that all traffic-accident deaths are followed by autopsies. That the family members are never asked for their consent. The body belongs to the coroner, not to the family.

We had cared for Kadian's body for fourteen years – every stubbed toe, every bruised knee. I gag, unable to speak. We have lost control. How is it possible that strangers were able to hack into my son's body? He is gone, we have utterly lost him.

From this point on, the image of his body with a Frankensteinian Y stitched thickly into his broadening chest repeatedly appears in my mind. It festers, clotting up my mental process, blocking the path for other, easier thoughts. This has happened before, but I had been able to find a way to unpick the knot, to get the thoughts flowing again. Not so with the autopsy.

I need to know what this means, what they did. I don't know why. I don't believe it is some vertiginous desire to throw myself into the pit of the macabre and unholy. I am attempting to establish the walls, floors, ceiling to the horror, for without them, the pain is unlimited and unbearable.

By this time I have moved therapists. Needing someone who could hand out drugs as well as advice, I closed the door properly on my lovely Greek therapist and asked around until I found someone suitable. The man I found was white-haired but young-faced. He exuded a confidence that said that he had seen a lot, but an alertness that said that he was keen to see more. I felt comfortable with him, that I could say anything. He also made me laugh, which I took as a good sign.

At my next appointment I ask my therapist, somewhat nervously, if he thinks it strange that I want to know more about Kadian's autopsy. He says it is healthy for me to want to understand.

I ask him a series of questions.

'Did they cut Kadian open?'

'Most likely yes,' he says. 'Sorry.' My stomach turns.

'And his head?'

'Yes, that as well. Sorry.'

'Would they have removed the organs?'

'Yes. Sorry,' he says again.

It is too awful to imagine.

'What did they do with the organs?'

'They would have returned them to the body cavity – it is required by law,' he says. And then, as an afterthought, he adds, 'Probably in plastic bags.'

Plastic bags. In my son's body. The thought disgusts me. This is too much. We keep talking, the conversation moving on from the autopsy to other matters, but my mind is snarled up with the plastic bags. Was it one bag per organ, or were the organs mixed together? Were the bags even biodegradable?

Am I losing my mind? Would people think I am mad to be asking such questions? A glutton for punishment, obsessive, encouraging a pathological impulse?

Yet it feels right, this quest for knowledge. If, as I have felt for some time, I am stranded in the well, inside a massive underground cavern, then such details – the plastic bags, the cause of death, the sweat dripping off the chin of the paramedic – are the damp craggy walls that I grope for in the dark. Solid rock, something to hold on to when all else is unstable, unreliable, treacherous.

*

There's an art to giving presents. It requires intelligence, generosity and empathy. It even requires timing. Kadian had been fantastic at it.

For my birthday one year, he told Deb that he had found a company who could print a photo of Duke on an iPhone case for my new phone. 'It will be great!' he said. 'Every time he takes a photo of someone they will look at the picture of Duke and smile!' But Deb said it was too expensive, and that I probably wouldn't like it. Not to be put off, Kadian persuaded Sam to go halves on the gift. Deb told Sam that it wasn't a good idea. But Kadian really wanted to buy the present so, in an uncharacteristically defiant move, he ordered it anyway. When I unwrapped the paper and saw its contents I shouted with delight and gave him a huge kiss. He resisted giving an I-told-you-so look to his mother and sister.

Or this example. One day, for no particular reason, Kadian mailed a one-dollar bill to Sam. Inside was a letter telling her how wonderful she was and how lucky he felt to have her as a sister.

Or this. To his French teacher, one year, he gave his grey metal stationery box, the same box that she had confiscated from him earlier in the year. To his English teacher, a Ms Jaffe, he gave a container filled with her favourite sweets. On the box he had written: 'Ashes of Grammatically Incorrect Students'.

And this. One Wednesday afternoon, Kadian was at home baking cookies with his friends. The phone rang. It was Sam. She said she was still at school and asked if someone could bring her a rain jacket. I looked outside at the rain pummelling the concrete patio. It was coming down so hard it was impossible to see the village hall across the street. I hesitated. 'I'll go,' said Kadian cheerily, and before anyone could stop him, he put on

Sam's raincoat, covered it with his own, attached his helmet, and rode through the storm to find his sister.

*

It is early September 2012, a few days into Sam's first term at Bedales. I am sitting on a chair in the garden reading a magazine when she returns home. Her hands are held behind her back.

'I have something for you,' she says, excitedly. 'It's a birthday present.'

A birthday present? I feel anger rising in my gut. My birthday had passed unnoticed a few days before. I had told anyone who asked that I didn't want presents, didn't want a fuss.

Sam walks up to me and hands me a plastic bag. Reaching inside I pull out a bubble-wrapped package. It has the weight and size of a teapot.

'One of the teachers gave it to me today. She says it's for you.' She pauses, unsure, then adds, 'It's from Kadian.'

Quickly unwrapping the parcel, I look at what is in my hands. It is a ceramic cube, painted white on the outside, black on the inside. In the interior stands a small black pedestal, on which sits a white ceramic Apple logo. To the left of the pedestal is a black cog, and I see attached to the outside of the cube there is also a white ceramic handle, as if to turn the apple. When looking at it from a distance the logo appears to be floating in mid-air. Above the cube are etched the words: 'Think Different'.

'Kadian made it in pottery class,' Sam tells me, looking over my shoulder. 'He spent the whole of last term working on it. He'd wanted to give it to you for your birthday.'

It is a brilliant, stunning, original gift, both intricate and witty. I feel sick. And then ashamed and confused by my response. It is too much. Too harsh a reminder that he could so easily have been here. That he should be here.

*

Almost as soon as Kadian died, we began discussing how to memorialise his life. A chance to create meaning where there was none.

I have an idea. I will email Apple, describe Kadian and his love of their products, his podcasts and videos, and ask if they can place an 'in memoriam' announcement on their website. Deb and Sam both agree it is a great plan, so I do it. As an illustration of my delusional state, I actually believe it will happen.

A few days later we receive an email response. They are very sorry, but as a matter of policy, this is not something Apple can do. Of course, I think to myself, there are thousands of Apple fans, how idiotic of me to think they could deliver this.

Then I keep reading. They have watched Kadian's YouTube videos and they wish to honour his memory by uploading his reviews as a series of podcasts on the iTunes Store. Kadian's work will gain global exposure through the site. They go on to say that while this proposal would not be a memorial in itself, Apple (and Jonathan Ive) feel that this is a far more appropriate way of genuinely honouring Kadian's life, his memory and his work.

Kadian would have been beyond excited by this, to have his work recognised by Apple and by Jonathan Ive himself, he would have been jumping and hollering with joy. Over the next few weeks we work with Apple to create an iTunes page dedicated to Kadian.

*

We are invited to my father's seventy-fifth birthday. It will be a 'small affair', not a party per se, more of a modest gathering.

I am confused. I want to go, to be a part of the group. Shouldn't we celebrate life as well as mourn the dead? But how can I even think of being joyful? Deb and Sam feel similarly torn.

We go back and forth. Should we go? Should we not? We change our minds five or six times in the week before the event. We tell my siblings that we might not be there. They reassure us that is fine . . . though say how wonderful it would be if we could make it. Eventually we choose to go.

We make it as far as a petrol station just south of Guildford, ten miles from our house. Deb is sobbing. Sam refuses to talk. She is listening to something on her iPhone. I am vacillating every few seconds between turning round and ploughing ahead. None of us are comfortable in the car. We feel disorientated. If time and space are overthrown, how is it possible to travel from one point to another? This is our first car journey together since Kadian died. The empty seat screams at us. We switch places a few times, finally opting for Deb in the driver's seat, Sam riding in the front passenger seat, me in the back. I phone to say that we are on our way.

My brother and sister are waiting for us outside my parents' house when we arrive. I wonder how long they have been there. We hug, they congratulate us, pleased that we have made it, I feel empty. Inside we receive more hugs. I find a safe place on a sofa in the corner, away from the group. Amanda sits next to me and asks how I am. I feel numb, bewildered, a stone on a beach waiting for the next wave. Sam is with her cousins, drinking Coca-Cola. Deb is surrounded by a group, talking fast, powering through it, transforming her grief and discomfort into hyper activity.

We are called to the kitchen where a cake is lit. 'Happy Birthday' is sung. No one mentions Kadian. I feel sick. Someone asks that the grandchildren gather round for a photograph. Sam hesitates, clearly uncomfortable. I am shocked. I walk into the living room. A family member follows me, putting an arm around my shoulders. 'I can't believe it either,' she says, knowing exactly why I walked out. 'I didn't think there should be a party. It's not right.'

It doesn't feel right. The party. The candles. The photograph. My son being dead.

I am still falling down the black well. How could we have been so stupid? We'd thought we should muscle through it, that we would feel good about ourselves for having attended the party. But we were wrong. We should never have come. The problem is, and it has taken me a long time to recognise this, I have lost my sense of judgement. Kadian died, suddenly, in front of me. Of course, when I put it that way, it seems obvious.

*

At night, Deb and I would tuck both the kids in. Sam would drift off quickly, but Kadian always took longer. When he was a toddler we called this 'fighting the dragon', as we watched him desperately try to fall asleep. Later we let him stay up reading, his light on past eleven o'clock, understanding that there was no point forcing him to sleep and that it was better for him to be in his bedroom than downstairs with us.

To help him relax, Deb often sat on his bed and talked about his day. This was a chance to unpack the emotions bottled up inside, the conflicts and tensions of the previous few hours. Normally, once he'd cleared his head he would fall asleep.

Theirs was a remarkable relationship. He had a strong need to spend time with his mother. At the age of three, he began playing the piano. At four he started with the Suzuki Method, which required that he and Deb practise together every day. This continued until he was ten, when Deb said he needed to practise by himself. He composed his own songs and performed them at school. But he hated practising alone and, after a while, he stopped playing.

They collected Lionel model trains and built a massive landscape out of plywood and polystyrene, around which trains puffed small clouds of white smoke. Kadian loved his lizards, but one of the main attractions was that his mother was prepared to feed them crickets, something that both he and I refused to do.

The two of them spent weeks together building elaborate Lego models. As he grew older Deb asked him why he kept asking for Lego sets for his birthday. He said, 'I didn't get them to do them on my own. I wanted them so that we could have more Kadian/Mum time.'

When the piano lessons had long stopped, the lizards and toads had all passed away, when the Lionel trains had been sold and the Lego stored away in boxes or handed down to a younger cousin, Kadian looked for another activity he could share with Deb. Finally, it dawned on him. Bicycles.

Before long they began discussing whether he could work at City Bikes, his mother's business in Washington.

*

My preoccupation with words continues.

What is the correct word for what I am experiencing? Is it grief, sadness, trauma, bewilderment? And what am I? I am a parent who has lost his child. I am bereaved, I am in mourning. Each of these words I tease over, allowing my mind to explore their nooks and crannies, tasting how they sound, how they feel. None is perfect.

A child who has lost his parents is an orphan. A husband or wife who has lost their partner, a widower or widow. I ask those close to me if they know of a word that describes me. No, they say, surprised.

Is it too awful to name? And if so, what does that mean?

I decide to find one. I go online and quickly discover some examples. In Hebrew, *horeh sh'khol* means 'parent who loses a child', and the Diyari, an Australian indigenous tribe, have the phrase *ngama mirka*, which means 'woman whose child has died' (*ngama* = breast/milk, *mirka* = hole). Yet these do not feel right to me. They are compound words. I need something more specific. I establish some rules: I am looking for a single word meaning 'parent who has lost a child' or 'parent whose child has died'.

I reach out further. I ask a translator, but she cannot think of a word. An expert in Eastern European languages tells me the same.

There are websites dedicated to this discussion; I find a couple of articles and even a book: *When There Are No Words*.

One academic proposes that we invent a word. She suggests *violmah*, which in Sanskrit means 'against the natural order'. But I don't know if a made-up word can carry enough significance.

Some people suggest that perhaps there are no words to describe a parent losing their child in any European language because child mortality is now so rare. But these languages were spoken when infant mortality was common. Two hundred thousand children died in Britain in 1905 alone. In France, Spain, Russia, Germany the numbers are similar. And yet none of these languages has a word.

Now a little obsessed, I begin to contact professors who specialise in exotic languages. Through chat rooms and blogs I locate some ethnolinguists who study in South-East Asia. Yet none of them knows of a word. I reach out to anthropologists who study remote peoples such as the !Kung in the Kalahari Desert, the Yanomami in Brazil, the Masai in Kenya. Again no words.

Then I am lucky. I discover three groups who do indeed have an appropriate word. In the Putijarra language, spoken by many of the indigenous people who live in the Australian Western Desert, the word *kampu* means 'bereaved parent', and can be used for either the mother or the father. In the Kaurna language, which is spoken by an indigenous group who live in the Adelaide Plains in South Australia, the word *murdanyi* refers to 'mother whose child has died', and *wikarnti* means 'father whose children are dead'. In the Chichewa language, which is spoken in Zambia and Malawi, the word *ofedwa* describes a bereaved parent.

I now have three words to describe myself, words that are actually used by people somewhere in the world today: *kampu*, *ofedwa* and *wikarnti*. I chose *kampu*, because it starts with the same two letters as Kadian's name.

I am a *kampu*. It feels strange, foreign, but isn't that exactly the point?

*

Small things and big things.

Sam's bag breaks. Cream-coloured and made from canvas, Kadian had made this satchel at school and given it to his sister. It was designed to be used as her school bag, with two black buckles at the front to prevent her books and files from falling out. He had even made a smaller inner sleeve to hold her much-loved iPad. A large black-and-white footprint was stencilled on the outside with the words, 'Walk whichever way you want'. It was crudely made, with rough stitching, but a more useful, thoughtful present there could not be.

A few weeks after Kadian died, Sam asks me about the bag. One of the buckles has ripped and many of the seams are fraying. She doesn't think it's right to put the bag on the shelf and stop using it, and she's worried that if she does nothing, the bag will get worse. Can we get it fixed?

But I am in no shape to help her, so I am grateful when the mother of one of Sam's school friends offers to take care of it. Two weeks later she returns the bag. The buckles have been reinforced, she says, but when the cobbler heard the bag's story, he told her he didn't want to go any further for fear of altering its appearance. It should be good for a while, he'd said.

A month or so later Sam brings me the bag again. There is now a large hole in one of the corners and the seams are unravelling at an alarming rate. By this time I am in better shape. I can drive up to the national speed limit without panicking, random interactions do not unsettle me and, while loud noises and quick movements still cause a disturbing rush of adrenalin or cortisol through my body, I feel confident that I will be able to help this time.

We drive to Haslemere and walk through a narrow alley to the main street. We find the cobbler opposite the deli. Pointing to the bag, I ask the woman at the counter if she thinks she could reinforce it, perhaps with leather, maybe some over-stitching? She looks at the bag. 'I'm not sure,' she says. 'Andrew will have to look at this. He's not here now, but if you give me your number he can give you a call.' I ask if he is close by. She says he's working on some projects around the corner, but that customers are not allowed in the workshop. 'Leave it with me,' she says. 'I'll make sure you hear from him soon.'

I give the woman my number, take a green ticket, say thank you and walk out. Sam is in the mood for shopping, so we go to a kitchen store and buy a couple of brightly coloured mugs. Since Kadian died I have been a bit of a pushover when it comes to her requests for new acquisitions.

Just as I am paying for the mugs my phone rings – it is the woman from the cobbler's shop. Andrew would actually like to see us now – could we go over? She gives me the address and a few minutes later we walk up another alley and duck our heads through a low wooden door. A smallish man with a scraggly beard and a black apron greets us, and introduces himself as Andrew. He leads us through a photography studio to a tiny, stone-walled room filled with sewing machines, leather samples and various items – bags, shoes, jackets, briefcases – in various stages of repair. 'It's warmer in here,' Andrew says. There was little light, and it was cramped and solitary. It was like a workshop from a Dickens novel.

'I've seen this before,' he says, turning the bag over in his hands. 'The trick is to make it stronger but keep the bag's look, isn't that right?' He asks Sam the question, not me, gaining him extra points. For the next ten minutes we discuss our options: using leather or canvas, patching the holes or adding a liner to the inside, reinforcing all or just some of the seams. He shows us some samples that lie curled up on a dusty shelf.

In the end Sam chooses the black leather and says that she would prefer not to have a lining, it would change the bag too much. As we leave Andrew says, 'It's not a typical job. I can't give a price, but I will be fair.'

Three weeks later I retrieve a message on my voicemail: 'Hi, this is Andrew. I've completed the repairs to the bag. In the end I went over all the seams, I reinforced the corners with leather strips, I added a leather patch to the hole. I didn't add a liner, the bag looks pretty much the same and I think that it will last a good long while without needing more work. I don't normally do this, but given what this is about, I don't want to charge you. I hope that's OK. The bag is ready for collection whenever you are.'

A little act of kindness, unprompted, spontaneous. A glimmer of light, from a random person touched tangentially by the colossal tragedy that we are living.

Small things and big things.

*

At the age of twelve Kadian started a summer job at City Bikes. It was never going to be easy working in his mother's business. The other staff were certain to think of him only as the boss's kid.

He began as a runner. His job was to push the bikes that had been checked in by customers across Euclid Street and down a short hill to the warehouse on 13th Street. Once inside the warehouse he had to steer the bikes past the mechanics and the racks they were working on to the back wall, and there hoist the bikes up onto a hook in the ceiling. Back and forth he would go each day, his thin legs running alongside the bikes down the hill. But he didn't really have the strength to be lifting large bikes, and often dropped them, scraping his arms and legs in the process. After a week or two he told me that he'd figured it out. Instead of lifting the back wheel, which was heavy and unwieldy, he lifted the front wheel, which was lighter and easier to control.

Eventually he was allowed to ride new inventory from the warehouse in Adams Morgan up to the Chevy Chase store. This was no easy task: the route ran eight miles along a bike trail, and the temperature outside was a sweltering 102 degrees. On his first trip Kadian arrived at the store tired and dripping with sweat, only to be told by the store manager, Wayne, that he'd brought the wrong bike. 'OK,' said Kadian, and wheeled the bike outside. 'I'm only kidding,' said Wayne, 'Come in and grab a drink.'

After a few more weeks, Kadian built up the confidence to start giving customers advice on the shop floor. 'The Bell helmet is much better than the Specialized,' he would offer, or, 'Those U-locks can be easily broken without a steel reinforce.' It occasionally got him into trouble with the tougher-than-nails store manager, Gin, who considered him far too young and inexperienced to be giving people advice. Gin told him that if he really wanted to work on the floor he would have to build his own bike. It was the best way to understand the mechanics, she said, to learn how everything worked together: how the gears powered the wheels, the cables feathered the acceleration, the tyres provided grip and traction.

It was the start of a new obsession.

*

The truth, and this is my deepest secret, is that our life was perfect before Kadian's death.

We had our health, and enough money. I was loved, and loved by those most important to me. I felt safe.

But now, this has gone. I live an imperfect life. Where before I could bounce back from a hardship, accommodate misfortune, like a rubber band stretched, but still whole, I am now undone, my ends frayed and hanging loose; perhaps I can be refastened, but I will never regain my former elasticity, my purpose forever questioned, in doubt.

My life is now tainted, stained, impure. I am broken.

*

I ask my therapist to explain what is happening inside my brain.

He says that the sudden death of a loved one can trigger a

specific chemical reaction. First, the hypothalamus in the brain emits corticotropin-releasing hormone (CRH), which in turn causes the pituitary gland to emit adrenocorticotropin hormone (ACTH) which then causes the adrenal gland, near the kidneys, to emit cortisol. It is this cortisol, he says, that has been flooding my body, making me feel alert, ready for action, hyper-vigilant.

I tell him that this explains why, when I'm in a coffee shop and the barista thumps the espresso handle against the machine, it feels like someone has clobbered me over the head with an axe. Why I can't walk along the pavement without jumping every time a car speeds past. Why I feel gripped by panic – heart racing, breathing hard, muscles tight – even when I'm sitting in my armchair in the living room reading a book.

The trick, he says, is to develop resilience. The idea being that humans have the capacity to bend in the face of severe pain and trauma, but not break.

'Yet I feel broken,' I tell him.

'That's not surprising,' he says, 'but I have never seen anyone confront their grief as you have done.'

I ask him if cortisol can damage the brain. He says that yes, it can. Some people do not have the capacity for resilience, while others face such extreme trauma that resilience is difficult if not impossible. In some cases the cortisol flood turns into a tsunami, which can destroy cells in the hippocampus and amygdala, regions involved with memory and emotion.

I have noticed that my cognitive functions have diminished since Kadian's death. My reflexes are slower now, my brain power weaker.

I am a worse driver. There have been a few times at T-junctions when I've pulled out too early, narrowly avoiding a car coming towards me. So far, I've been lucky, and there haven't been any accidents. Though my already racing heart races faster.

My eyesight has also dramatically worsened. This may be a coincidence. I am at that age now, in my mid-forties, when many people find themselves holding their reading material at arm's length.

But I find reading itself difficult. I can process a paragraph, but find it next to impossible to read an entire chapter in one go, let alone a whole book. My mind simply stalls. Perhaps this is a refusal to let go of reality, an emotional block, or a failure of cognitive power, the inability to grasp complex concepts spun out across scores of pages. Either way I try not to panic. Is this what they mean by 'acceptance' when it comes to grief, one of the five stages, acceptance of my diminished abilities, the diminishing of my powers and skills, the tumbling of my talents?

And my memory is failing. Whereas in the past I could have told you precisely what I did during the previous week or even month, now entire time periods appear blank, particularly in the weeks after Kadian's death.

I think it unlikely that I am non-resilient, given what I have had to overcome in my life, but perhaps the trauma of seeing my child killed before my eyes is such that even the most hardy, the toughest among us, would break.

Broken, unable to spring back. The supplest of branches will snap eventually, if enough force is applied.

It helps to talk to my shrink. To give voice to my greatest fears. It makes me feel a little less mad, a little less of a freak. I am feeling these things because of the way I am wired, the way that we are wired. He also gives me hope. Just perhaps, I think, if he knows why I am feeling this way, he will also know how to help me not to feel this way.

*

As he approached his thirteenth year, the question arose as to whether Kadian would have a bar mitzvah. I'd completed my bar mitzvah, as had my brother, father, and all my cousins. Being Jewish was part of our family identity. My grandparents had been forced to flee Nazi Germany in the 1930s. They had smuggled the family Torah out of Berlin and this had formed the basis of a new synagogue in north London. Being Jewish was important to us.

But Kadian was not someone who blindly adopted another's opinions. He had to work it out for himself.

For months I badgered him about starting his Hebrew lessons. I tried to lock him in by setting a date for the big day. I even tempted him with the prospect of a mountain of presents. During these moments Deb would look at me like I was a witch doctor from an exotic tribe. She had given up on the idea of religion long ago and felt I was being too pushy.

At first, he went along with the idea but then, when he couldn't put it off any longer, he told us that he didn't want to do it. He just didn't see the point. He said that he didn't believe in God, he didn't buy all the old stories he'd read in the Bible, he couldn't understand the Hebrew he was learning, and had no plans to move to Israel.

The only concern he had, he told us as tears slid down his face, the one thing that prevented him from making a decision earlier, was that he worried he would be shunned by the family if he didn't go through with the ceremony.

I backed down, and quickly realised how mistaken I'd been. Suddenly, and belatedly, I grasped his maturity. I told him that I gave him my support, one hundred per cent.

From this point, whenever I was asked by family members about his bar mitzvah I told them that he had chosen not to have one. It was through this decision-making, through standing up for himself, that he had become an adult.

*

Keith, the headmaster at Bedales, calls us. He suggests that we meet to discuss holding a memorial ceremony for Kadian at the school.

A few days later we are in his office overlooking a green courtyard, dotted with apple trees and a couple of bronze life-sized horse sculptures. There are six of us, Keith, Dominic the deputy headmaster, Graham, our neighbour and a teacher at the school, Deb and myself.

It is a difficult situation for many reasons. Deb and I are unmistakably raw, vulnerable, hypersensitive to any misspoken word and, while presenting ourselves as wanting to be in charge of any decision, clearly mentally challenged, struggling with details, unable to organise any event. The headmaster has his own problems. Kadian died during the holidays, the students have not yet processed the news as a group, and for the vast majority this would be the first friend or acquaintance who has died.

Keith offers to host a memorial service at the school. He

generously invites all of our friends and family to attend, and says that we would have final say on the format and programme.

Graham will put together a possible outline and book the school's best venue, the Olivier Theatre. We will reconvene in a week's time.

A week later there is a letter waiting for us on the doormat: Graham's outline for the memorial service. We baulk at his suggestions: church music, a hymn, a few readings. It all seems so un-Kadian.

Graham's letter leaves us uncertain how to proceed. We don't want to sound ungrateful, but we have to get this right. There is a genuine conflict here: the school wants to provide pastoral care for the students, many of who have just learned of Kadian's death. A traditional memorial ceremony is the best option for them. We, on the other hand, want to celebrate his life, bring a sense of wonder and joy to the group, propel people forward. Perhaps they know what's best for their students, but we know Kadian. The conflict both distresses and overwhelms us.

We call my aunt who reminds us this is important, there will only be one memorial service for Kadian, that we have to push through our discomfort. She will be there to support us all the way.

A month of indecision goes by. We become increasingly concerned that we won't be ready in time. The anxiety adds to our already fragile state.

The school's head of drama drops by our house for a cup of tea. We ask him what we should do and he says we can do anything we like. 'Even if it's crazy?' Deb asks. He laughs kindly. 'What's crazy? You've just lost your son. You can do anything you want.'

A cloud lifts, we can suddenly see clearly. We realise that we don't want a memorial service – filled with dry speeches, hymns and dour faces – we want a show. Something that will reflect the colour and richness of Kadian's life.

Fortunately, the school is sensitive to our ideas. Having compiled a shortlist of songs that Kadian liked and those that we think will be good to dance to, we give the school a selection that we wish to include. They agree to everything. When they suggest that the choir sings a couple of classical pieces, both of which have ties to Kadian, we gratefully accept. In this way, and with extreme care, we negotiate a programme that suits us both.

The school finds out which students want to participate and then helps facilitate their performance. These students meet with teachers over the course of the next few weeks, remembering their time with Kadian and discussing possible ideas.

Sam says she wants to participate, and room is found for her in the programme. She creates a slideshow of images of herself and Kadian – in front of the Colosseum in Rome, at the Tower of London, next to Duke as a puppy, by the river near our house – most have Kadian's arm around Sam.

Deb and I both know we want to say something, but we are confused, blocked. What do you say about a teenager's life? It's not like they have lived sixty, seventy, eighty years, built up a lifetime's worth of achievements. Should we speak separately? Should we edit each other's words? Should we speak at the start or end of the event? What will have the biggest impact? Do we even want an impact? And then I worry that only a few people will attend, that the room will be marked by empty seats, that it will dishonour Kadian. I send out reminder emails, makes lists of those I know are coming. Deb and I talk about this, at some length. She tries to reassure me. 'We have done all we can,' she says. 'The important people will be there.'

The night arrives.

It is raining lightly outside. We walk the short distance down the road and through the school car park to the theatre. Having greeted a few people who have gathered on the wet pavement, we go inside. I am aware that I'm nervous, worried that we will blow this one chance. That people will walk away saying 'that was nice' or 'that was quite moving', and that we will have missed our opportunity to celebrate all that was unique and extraordinary about Kadian.

As we enter the theatre everyone is handed a 'Kadian Box', a small silver tin box whose contents Debora has somehow produced in time for the event.

Sitting down at the front of the auditorium I look carefully at the box. On the outside is a picture etched in purple of Kadian's bicycle leaning against a tree. Inside there are seven double-sided printed cards. On the first are written the following words: 'The extreme distance that Kadian travelled – from full-throttled happiness and engagement in life to sudden death on 25 July, has left thousands on both sides of the Atlantic in shock. Death is not the reward for such happiness. How is it possible that it be Kadian? Joyous, vibrant, alive . . . cheerful and charming Kadian? As we can only imagine what Kadian's future may have become, we've included these memory cards to share the parts that make the whole of this beautiful young man.'

The other six cards focus on separate parts of Kadian's life: his love of nature, his obsession with Apple and its founder Steve Jobs, his family and his dog Duke, Bedales, his support for an anti-bullying campaign, cycling. Inside the box there is also a small bag of wild-flower seeds for people to take away and sow, as well as a purple bracelet with his name. There is also a full-colour picture of the four of us, smiling at the camera, together.

Looking around the theatre I am relieved to see that it is packed. There are over three hundred people here: the extended family, our friends, Kadian's friends, Sam's friends. And there are others, people from the village, parents of kids from school. Work colleagues.

The lights dim and from the darkness come the mournful voices of the school choir singing Brahms's 'Ye Now Have Sorrow'. The pace of the music is slow, sombre. It unites us, it makes us forget our preoccupations, our outside lives. We focus on Kadian.

As they finish, the audience claps, and the choir is replaced by nine of Kadian's friends, dressed in jeans and brightly coloured T-shirts – yellow, blue, green, red. Bruno Mars's upbeat 'Count on Me' booms from the speakers: 'You can count on me, like one, two, three, I'll be there . . .' His friends jump backwards off benches and roll around the floor with arms gaily waving. They give each other piggybacks and race each other around the stage. The mood is contagious.

At the end of the song, the kids sit on a bench at the side of the stage and, along with the audience, watch a short film that is projected on a large screen hanging from the ceiling. It is the film Kadian made with his friend Finn: they are jumping backwards off walls, steps, statues.

A new song plays: 'I Love My Mac' by Daphne Kalfon. Another group of Kadian's friends enter the stage. In their arms they each hold a MacBook and as the song kicks in they dance and twirl to the catchy beat, teenagers waltzing with their computers. Then the house lights are turned down and the kids hold out their MacBooks in outstretched arms, open the lids, and dance in concentric circles, emitting a bluish glare which illuminates the entire theatre. It is magical.

We then watch another video, this one made by Kadian's school friends, in which they share their feelings looking straight to camera. They laugh at him messily eating popcorn in the cinema. They repeat in-jokes which a few in the audience laugh at but bemuse the rest of us. They say they miss him. Then they present a montage of photographs that Kadian has taken of them, an us-watching-you-watching-us sequence. The images are beautifully shot; I hadn't known that Kadian had such a great eye.

Then it is our turn. Realising that we could not perform without interruptive tears we have asked my cousin James and his wife Kate to read our words. They walk up onstage and sit on the bench. Above them hangs a large tree branch, a canopy of protective green leaves.

Slowly, deliberately, James and Kate speak, taking their time, using pauses and small body movements – a shuffle forward, a touch of the arm, sitting more upright – to emphasise the words:

> Deb: We decided to walk to Hawkley Pub today. I fell behind as I usually do, and imagined you fell back with me . . . as you always did. As we start up Shoulder of Mutton I want to reach for your outstretched hand. It was always there, helping me with my appalling balance. We climb to the Poet's Stone. You should be here now, on the ground, chewing rye grass, stroking Duke as he gently paws you.
>
> Thomas: I miss your face. Your smiley face. Your chiselled chin. I miss your left hand holding. Pointy elbow right. Spooning sugary cereal to your mouth.

Deb: I had tea with our neighbour Susie. I remembered you stopped by her house to borrow an egg two weeks ago. That's when you were real – when you baked things like apple pie and chocolate muffins. Now I feel pretend.

Thomas: I miss your deep brown thick hair. You flick across your brow. Once, twice, out of your eyes. Oh your eyes. How I miss these too. Blue grey. Colour changing. Keen welcoming. Eager for stare competition. Hungry to see the world.

Deb: I see this . . . your happy face, riding by Sam and me on our morning walk to Dunhurst School. You pedal past us, dressed in your wool pea coat, backpack strapped over your shoulders, yell 'Love you' and disappear into the wind.

Thomas: You loved to weird us out. Rolling your eyes back. Whites showing. Or cross them to a point. 'Please stop that,' we'd say. Now I think, Please don't.

Deb: I mowed the lawn today. The last time you cut it you insisted on leaving a circled patch of something that was clearly a grass threat. But now that patch of grass has flowered into tiny, thick yellow petals and a village of bumblebees, and I'm afraid of what I'll miss without your magic touch.

Thomas: I miss your hands. Your giving, helping hands. Flying over the keyboard. Rolling out the dough. Pushing the mower up the hill. Making good-luck cards for your sister. Bringing me the perfect caffè latte.

Deb: I couldn't wait to get home from work. I'd see your head in the window, you peeking out, whispering 'Mumma'. I'd try to hide my pleasure that you were up past your bedtime, come tuck you in, and we'd go through the ritual of our special kiss – left cheek . . . right cheek . . . nose . . . forehead . . . chin. You never outgrew it. You'd pat your bed and say 'come lie down with me,' and I'd say 'You need to sleep,' you'd pat it again and say 'Please' and we'd lie, our heads together and you'd say 'Tell me about your day'.

Thomas: I miss the small freckle. On your right hand's second finger. Hidden inside. Just like your sister's. I miss your feet. Narrow, strong. Carrying you. Unshoed across paths many.

Deb: Do you remember that family camping trip with the prehistoric green bug? We were on the banks of the Shenandoah. The trees were blanketed with fireflies and sparkled like fairy lights. Your sister woke, screaming. A fist-sized insect had crawled over her. She refused to go back to sleep. Without being asked, you grabbed a lantern, took her hand, reassured her and led her to your tent. Ten minutes later we heard you both laughing as you cast animal shapes into shadows.

Thomas: I miss your long legs. Often crossed. At table. In bed. On sofa. Skinny yet powerful. Skiing hiking cycling. I miss your slender waist. Trousers slipping down. Exposing boxers. Thick-striped. I miss your acrobatic lips. Forming comic shapes. Making us howl with laughter.

Deb: This week one of your primary school classmates wrote to us. She said that all she had to do was ask you for your best Pokémon cards and you would give them to her. She said you did it because it made you happier than keeping them and that it is something she would always remember.

Thomas: I miss your body moves. Head bobbly round and round. As if detached. Arms shaking from shoulders. Like two thick ropes aquiver. Legs folded lotus-style. Walking on knees. 'Look at me, Dad,' you'd say. 'Look at me.'

Deb: Alice wrote today, saying that you were such a bright, sweet kid. She remembers when she gave you a present of colourful paper and you immediately fashioned a piece into a thank-you note for her. She says that she's kept this paper, a treasure. You were so considerate that way – always in tune with other people, always so generous.

Thomas: I miss the peach fuzz. Growing beneath your nose. Sign of manhood approaching. Your adolescent smell. Masked by powerful deodorant. I miss the crown of your head. So close to mine. 'I'm going to look down. At your bald spots, Dad.' But now. Never inching higher.

Deb: I saved a card you mailed to me one day. It was random. You were ten. And you used your very special Dolphin stationery. No special occasion. It read, 'I am sorry this took so long to get to you but I've been forgetting to find time in your day to go running with me and Duke. You give 100 per cent attention to my train and make me delicious breakfast all while working. Only a perfect mother could do that. Kads.'

Thomas: I miss your knobbly knees. Crashing into my belly. 'Time to wake up, my Dads.' I miss your gorgeous ears. Long pierced. No longer adorned. Unable to hear high frequencies. Yet highly attuned. To song, emotion, mirth.

Deb: And this handmade card from you as well. 'Dear Mum, I hope you have a wonderful 46th year. Thanks so much for being my loving Super Pooch for 11½ years. And don't tell the others but I will be on your side in Paint Ball. Once again, have a wonderful day and may all your wishes come true. Love Kadian.'

Thomas: I miss your tears. For happy endings. At sad stories. In your own anger. I miss your many voices. Not yet unsung. But unsung.

Deb: My last goodbye before you left . . . I rumpled that lovely thick brown hair of yours and we share the ritual word exchange you started when you were four – 'Best mother in the world,' you say. 'Best son in the world,' I say. And rather than our ritual goodnight kiss – left cheek, right cheek, nose, forehead, chin – I kiss your forehead as I am not tucking you in.

Thomas: Most of all. I miss your body against mine. In standing cuddle. Or couch embrace. Relaxed secure. Together. As if nothing would ever change.

As I listen to their words, and even though I know them so well, I cry uncontrollably. Shoulders heaving, palms covering my face as if that could stem the tide.

Towards the end of the celebration Keith, the headmaster, stands and takes to the stage. Wearing a dark suit and white shirt, he removes a stack of cards from his jacket pocket. Behind him a giant photograph of Kadian is projected onto the screen. From the cards, Keith starts reading the testimonies of Kadian's teachers. At first I am concerned that this speech is too stiff, too formal, but before long the audience is rocking with laughter. It is a welcome relief after the intensity of the previous minutes.

His geography teacher reports that Kadian 'found a way to bring Apple into every conversation'. His drama teacher says that 'Kadian is the class clown . . . but in a good way.' His music teacher explains that 'the early stages of singing with a broken voice can be a frustrating period . . . but not so for Kadian'. His chemistry teacher says 'Kadian sometimes misses the point of an activity and produces a piece of work which is in essence good . . . but answers none of the right questions.' His maths teacher remembers, 'Kadian was bright, enthusiastic, a very liked member of the class, he enjoyed pointing out the differences between American and British terminology, for example, "It is not a trapezium, it is a trapezoid!"'

Keith pauses, and then become more serious. 'On a personal level,' he says looking at the audience, the report cards now at his side, 'I miss his smiling face in our few shared English lessons. I miss the chats we used to have walking into school down the path in the morning. I miss his easy, natural manner, which treated me more as a fellow human being than as a headmaster. Loyal, colourful, engaging, generous-spirited, good-humoured, inquisitive, lively minded, ingenious, idealistic, and determined to embrace life's opportunities, Kadian was in his element at Bedales. Whether it be through our memories of these qualities, or his smile, or his laughter, or that glint in his eye, we will remember him. We were privileged to know him.'

Another of Kadian's friends, a girl called Daisy, walks onto the stage. She is surrounded by all the performers, forty people in all. Standing next to the bench, she sings 'Beautiful Boy', the song that Sam and Dominic wrote in the days after Kadian died.

It is an extraordinary finale, one that brings all the event's elements together. The cast have tears in their eyes, as do we.

And there it ends. The audience claps and then looks around. The performers are still on the stage. Deb, Sam and I stand, coats in hand, and start to leave. Yet it is obvious that something must be said.

Deb stops, turns to the performers onstage. 'This is such a beautiful gift that you have given us. Kadian loved Bedales, his friends, his teachers. From the moment he arrived, he hit the ground running and didn't stop,' she says, through her tears. 'Kadian will continue to be with us all. Thank you for being with us today.' And with that, we walk out.

I am exhausted, my circuits too blown to talk. Holding Sam's arm in my left hand, and Deb's in my right, I walk out of the theatre, eager for a glass of whisky and respite at home. I am drained, but love him even more.

*

My phone rings. 'Hi, this is Audrey.'

Audrey, who is Audrey? I don't know any Audreys.

'Hi. This is Thomas,' I say, playing for time.

In recent days I have realised that my short-term memory has worsened and I don't want to embarrass myself by not recognising someone I should. The voice on the other end of the line starts again.

'We've set the date for the inquest at the end of April, but we wanted to make sure that you wouldn't be away.'

Inquest. A word I never thought I would come into personal

contact with. A word you hear on the television news or read in the paper. A word associated with murder, a major crime, an opportunity for the powers that be to establish why something dreadful had happened to some nice people. It conjures up scenes of grieving family members, gathered in their Sunday best, in front of some municipal building, their lawyers speaking on their behalf, from prepared notes, sharing their anguish at the misfortune in which they are now embroiled. This was never meant to be part of my story, so carefully imagined, constructed, performed. How can this be? The very word is anathema to me. This feels like the opposite of a 'quest', it feels like a journey to hell.

I tell Audrey that I think it will be fine, without looking at my calendar – after all, what else will we be doing? We are, as Deb said to me recently, full-time grieving parents. Unable to work, unable to socialise, without the energy to shop for groceries or to carry out home improvements, our lives are one hundred per cent about the loss of Kadian. If an inquest is part of the job description, of course we will be there.

Our lawyers tell us that the owner of the bike shop will be there, giving evidence. How will I respond? I wonder. Will I sit meekly in my chair, hands folded, looking away? Will I be seized by rage, leap across the room, fingers locked around his neck, squeezing? Most likely I will be racked by grief, sobbing unstoppably, embarrassed by my emotional display, wanting only to leave, for it to be over with, to get home to my dog and my bottle of whisky.

I have just finished John Grisham's *A Time to Kill.* The story revolves around a father on trial for killing the two men who brutally raped and beat his young daughter. Interestingly, to me at least, the question of restraint and due process receives scant attention in the book. Grisham assumes that we, the reader, agree that it is acceptable, commendable even, to seek revenge on your child's assailants. And I wonder why I haven't acted. Is it cowardice not to seek vengeance? What would a real man do? I have spent much of my working life tracking down those who do wrong, passing judgement on them, working with others to mete out consequence. Why not now?

What will I do if the legal process fails to act? What if my son has died, and the man who worked on his bike suffers no consequence? What if he if allowed to continue working on bikes, to perpetuate his trade? What is the justice system finds that he is not at fault? Will I sit outside his business, rain or shine, placard held aloft, declaring his misdeeds, calling for the shop to be shut down? Tolerated for a short while, perhaps even sympathised with by some of the locals. I might even receive some positive attention from the local media, but after some weeks, I would be asked to move on by the police and community, grown tired of the drama and the disruption.

None of this is going to happen, I know. My fears are all precisely that, fears. Our lawyers have told us that an inquest does not establish blame, it will not accuse anyone of being at fault, all that can be hoped for is that a cause can be determined: Kadian did not try and stop himself, or Kadian did try and stop himself but his brakes failed.

It will be fine, I tell myself. But I'm not sure.

*

There are not many days left in this journal. I want to slow these stories down. To savour each moment. Delay what's coming. Delay the end. So I'll jump back a few months.

We decided to make marmalade together, because Deb loves it. Because we knew it would make her happy. She was in Washington, working.

It was January, the air outside was cold, the sky overcast; we spent most of our time inside. But January also meant Seville orange season.

We purchased the oranges from the supermarket, along with four kilograms of sugar, a bag of lemons, and a pack of pectin to make the mixture good and thick. Back at home we set to work. I readied the glass containers, finding old jam jars stored at the back of cupboards, cleaning them in the sink, sterilising with boiling water.

Kadian meanwhile had the arduous task of preparing the fruit. First he peeled the oranges and lemons, then sliced the peel with a sharp knife on a large wooden chopping board. It was monotonous work. Taking his time, he built one, then two tall mounds of brightly coloured strips.

To the huge steel pot of boiling water, we added the sugar, the sliced peel and the pectin. Into this we dangled a cheese cloth full of the separated pulp. Having been warned that the frothing liquid would burn if any of it splattered onto his skin, Kadian started skimming the white scum that began to form on the surface.

Then we waited for the sugary mixture to thicken. Every so often we tested it on a chilled plate to see if it was ready, but each time our efforts slid away. We waited some more. Then, at last, the treacly goo was set and we poured it into labelled jars. It glistened, a translucent orangey-brown bottle of goodness. I smiled. Kadian smiled back. We both knew how good this would taste on a thick wedge of buttered bread.

Kadian carried the jars of marmalade, now sealed and hot to the touch, to the kitchen table and arranged them in a triangle shape. His mother would find them when she arrived home that afternoon.

And I wonder, will I ever make marmalade again?

*

A brown envelope arrives from our lawyers. Inside are the statements of the witnesses who will appear before the inquest.

So here it is. At last I will get to see things from other people's point of view. For so long I have been trapped in my own, singular perspective. The images have solidified, the short snippets of visual and oral memory, replayed over and over again in my mind, have become established neural pathways etched into my mental circuitry, like water cutting its way into a riverbed. I am hoping that these other viewpoints will create new avenues for my mind to wander along, to remap the most painful of my memories.

Perhaps at last I will find out what actually happened on that day. What caused the accident? Why did the brakes not work? Why did he not slow down?

I read the witness statements. The police forensic expert says the front brake failed, the pinch bolt that held the cable that held the brakes was loose. The bike shop owner says it wasn't his fault. He didn't work on the front brake. Though he did admit that Kadian had brought his bike in for repair less than four hours before the fatal accident. A driver close to the scene of the accident says the van driver was not speeding.

I read other statements. Kadian's friend Rori, who says she remembers Kadian asking the bike shop owner to look at the brakes. My friend Dominic, who has a receipt that says that the 'brakes' were fixed and that the day after the accident the bike shop owner told him that he had fixed both front and rear brakes. My sister and her friend who said that they saw the A4 from a distance and had plenty of time to brake.

None of this is new. I have heard it already from the police officer who took my statements months ago. What is new is to hear the witnesses describe the moment of the accident.

There is a Mr Long, who works at the water plant next to the path we cycled down. He was in his car, on his way home, waiting to turn left onto the A4 when he saw Kadian coming down the track 'like a bat out of hell'. He saw him hit by a white van, knocked about twenty feet down the road, ending up face down on the ground.

There is a Mr Witt, also in a car and on his way back home. He was waiting on the other side of the A4, waiting for the traffic to clear, when he saw someone on a bicycle hit by the van and thrown into the air 'like a rag doll'. A rag doll. Not a young man full of life and future and promise. A rag doll.

And the van driver. Finally I get to hear from the van driver. He is called Mr White. At the end of a long day, after driving from Wiltshire to London and back, dropping off one last delivery for his boss, he too is heading home. Suddenly he hears a crack, his windscreen is smashed, and out of the corner of his eye he sees a person flying through the air. My son.

This is all hard enough to read. But nothing compares to the pathologist's report which hides at the back of the bundles of papers. Here I will be able to see exactly what happened during the autopsy. I could stop here, perhaps I should, but I don't. I want to know every detail, hoping that through knowledge will come a sense of control.

The pathologist sums up Kadian's appearance taken during an external examination: abrasions on the forehead measuring 3 x 5 cm. A complex abrasion on the chest measuring 22 x 29 cm 'consistent with gravel lacerations from being dragged along the road'.

I read on. The report includes a toxicology statement. My heart skips a beat. An avalanche of thoughts, mostly driven by insecurities, tumble through my brain. Am I about to be told some secret about my son? Some shocking revelation? Surely I would have known if Kadian was doing drugs or getting drunk. Of course I would know. But don't all parents claim to be surprised when they learn about their children's vices? I immediately feel disloyal for these thoughts and force myself to read the results. Not surprisingly, there are no traces of alcohol or drugs in his body. For this small blessing I am grateful and feel relief.

I keep going, and move on to the heading I fear most: 'Internal examination'. Bracing myself, my eyes scan over the sentences: 'The appearance of the body was commensurate with the chronological age . . . The pulmonary valve was normal . . . the anatomy of the great vessels was normal'. Then this sentence, 'The heart weighed 315g and was of normal size and shape.'

My son's heart weighed 315g. This is something I never expected to know. Never wanted to know. To know this, the pathologist must have cut the heart from his chest and taken it to a scale. The thought of this makes my body buzz, I feel dizzy, nauseous.

The report continues, describing the weight, colour and shape of the lungs, liver, pancreas, kidneys. All normal. And then the brain. Which weighed 1336g.

I imagine the pathologist cutting the brain out of Kadian's head, carrying it in his latex-gloved hands, placing it on a stainless-steel dish, and weighing it. These are impossible images. This is the brain that made me laugh, that chose to make his mother coffee in the morning, that taught his sister how to use an iPod. This is the brain that could get on the phone and problem-solve any issue with a customer service representative, whether they be from Bangalore or Boston. This is the brain that sought comfort by holding onto a black-and-white stuffed orca each night. This is the brain that was destined to do extraordinary and wonderful things in this world. This is the brain that was 'diffusely swollen' with a 'slight flattening of the pons', the brain that had experienced traumatic impact against the windscreen, dramatically increasing the pressure in the skull, crushing the cortex down into the only place available, the *foramen magnum*, the wide hole at the bottom of the skull, through which the spinal cord reaches the brain. The brain stem that had been compressed, known as 'coning', which caused instant death.

I search the Internet and find a study conducted by a professor at the University of Basel which found that the average brain weight in over eight thousand autopsies of adult men was 1336g. Precisely the same as Kadian's brain. Surely this cannot be a coincidence. Does this mean that the pathologist faked the results, that he didn't cut the brain out after all? And then I realise how ridiculous this sounds. That my emotional response says more about me than about the pathologist. I clearly hate the idea of the autopsy and am grasping for a way to make myself believe it never happened.

I turn to the last page of the autopsy: Kadian's death was unnatural. There is no question about that.

*

Whenever I tell people about the inquest they warn me how awful it is going to be. I must brace myself for the cold objectivity of the law, they caution. 'Make sure there are people around you who can lend support,' they say. Never have I been forewarned in this way, with such unanimity and vehemence.

How bad can it be? I think to myself. I have read the witness statements. I have even looked at the pathology report. Perhaps other people are shocked by what they hear at an inquest. I am prepared, I will not be surprised. And, in terms of the emotional Richter scale, nothing can compare to the loss of Kadian. I am confident I will be able to handle it.

We decide to drive to the coroners' court, just the three of us – Deb, Sam and me. It will be together time, a chance to bond before the storm.

Sam's participation has been controversial. Should a fourteen-year-old attend the inquest of her brother? Is it better for a teenager to be a participant, to witness the unfiltered facts and complex interpretations, or to avoid the proceedings, pursue a 'normal' teenage life of school, television and friendships? In the end, we warned her of the possible consequences and, trusting in her judgement, left the decision to her.

The inquest is to be held in Salisbury, about thirty miles south of Marlborough. The courthouse itself is a white Georgian building on the corner of two narrow roads a few hundred yards from the city's main square. Inside we are greeted by Audrey, the coroner's assistant – white shirt, narrow shiny black trousers, all bustle and business, she looks like a middle-aged waitress in a hurry to serve the next table.

'Before I show you the court,' she says, 'I should tell you that Kadian's bike is inside.'

Kadian's bike? For a brief moment I feel the surge of rising hope. Kadian's bike, is he nearby? Can I see him? Then I realise it's his damaged bike, the one that he died on, the one that the police have kept in storage since the accident.

The courtroom fills up. Behind me sit friends and family members, who have taken time out of their busy lives to be here for the next two days. For this I am appreciative. They will serve as emotional support, available for interim discussions, hugs. They are also here as a sign of respect for the seriousness of the matter. A young child has died, suddenly, terribly; this is the state's process, they should be here as witnesses, demonstrating that they care, that this is important.

In front of me sits our lawyer, Jeremy Hyam, a sharp-tongued and quick-witted barrister from London. I'm glad he's on our side. To his left sits the owner of the bike shop – Acceler8 Motoring & Leisure Shop Ltd – and his barrister. Worried that I may want to punch him, or worse, I have asked my friends to intervene if necessary. Seeing him I realise that I need not have worried. I look over. His eye twitches; he appears weak, unkempt, diminished.

Next to me sits Sam. She is organising her belongings into a neat symmetric formation, notepad, pens, iPhone, book. On the other side of Sam sits Deb.

A few minutes later we stand as the coroner enters. He is wearing a blue pinstriped suit, a blue tie dotted with small crowns, and is clutching a stack of folders and sheets of paper. He looks grim, sour, efficient.

He explains that the purpose of the inquest is to determine the cause of Kadian's death. It is not his task to apportion blame, it's to find facts and record them in an official verdict. The inquest will take two days, he says, there will be fifteen witnesses, including the police, experts and those who observed the collision. Each time he mentions that Kadian died he pauses for a beat and wraps the facts in a bow of pathos – 'Kadian's tragic death' or 'when Kadian sadly died' – telegraphing his sympathy and compassion to those before him.

Our barrister stands and says we hope the coroner will see that Kadian died because of negligence on the part of a bicycle mechanic, and that he will recommend that in future bicycle mechanics should be qualified. The coroner barks that he does not believe in a 'nanny state', and that small businesses should not be subject to further regulation.

He calls his first witness, PC Trafford, who presents a video of himself riding down the path towards the A4.

'So tell us what we are seeing,' the coroner says.

I watch the video; the trees and bushes rush past, the narrow muddy trail swallowed up by the speeding bike. I recognise this place, from my dreams, from that day. But it is all too fast. It is over too quickly – woods, the opening onto the final slope, the A4. The bike stops. This is not how I remember it. In my memory it is much slower, time spreads out, the bumps and jostles of the rocks and stones, the turns of the path, the angle of the slope.

'I will ask Mr Harding to take the stand.'

I am nervous. Nervous that he will ask me a trick question. Nervous that I will not do justice to Kadian, for Kadian. Nervous that I will not be able to cope.

At first the coroner affects a tone of camaraderie, of one parent talking to another, swapping fond stories of their children. He asks me about Kadian, his love of bikes, his interest in Apple products, his joy at swinging from a rope into a stream, his eagerness to climb trees.

I take my time, making sure I only give answers that I am sure of, challenging the coroner if I don't agree or understand his question. He asks about the moments after the accident, when I found Kadian on the road. I refuse to answer. I don't want Sam or Deb to hear this, certainly not here, in court. The coroner agrees, reluctantly, to move on to other questions.

Then he turns adversarial, harsher: Tell me about the purchase of the bike. Tell me about the assembly. The final ride. Kadian's mental state. The conditions. The route.

Of all the memories of Kadian's death this is the one that has been tucked away. This hour and a quarter is buried deep. At least from the readily accessible part of my brain. Maybe, if I dig hard enough, I can repeat each and every anguished moment.

The coroner gets more aggressive. He asks me to look at a specification sheet he has found on the Internet. It says that Kadian's tyres were designed for commuting and, by implication, were not for use off-road. He asks me if I had a compass, and if not, why not. He chides me for getting lost that day – why didn't I use the position of the sun to determine that we were following an incorrect route? Was Kadian the kind of boy who would race his father down a hill? Did I accompany Kadian to the bike shop? Had I chosen the bike shop? Did I ask a bike shop to conduct a pre-delivery inspection of the bike before I let Kadian ride it?

My worst fears are realised. He appears to have determined

the account of the inquest before hearing the testimony. He is going to blame me.

Finally, he is finished. Our barrister asks some follow-up questions which reveal a greater truth: that Kadian had taken his bike to Acceler8 to have the brakes adjusted a few hours before the accident, that both brakes had failed. Not because we lacked a compass or I couldn't read the sun. Not because Kadian was an overexcited teenager racing his dad down the hill, because he didn't.

I feel exhausted. My muscles ache and tremble. I am quickly surrounded by my friends and family. They take me outside and feed me sandwiches and chocolate. They tell me I have done well, I performed with honour and dignity, that I held my own, that I remained remarkably cool and objective. They criticise the coroner for the brutality of his questions and for his lack of compassion.

Numbly, I eat my chocolate bar.

*

I see Kadian during the inquest. He is with me. Scruffy jeans, button-down shirt, bare feet.

An octagonal glass dome covers the opening which has been cut out of the middle of the ceiling. He sits on the narrow ledge that runs along the bottom edge of the octagonal glass skylight, his long spindly legs dangling down, smiling warmly, a little mischief in his eyes. 'Don't take them seriously, Dad, they're idiots. We both know what really happened.'

He is here. I point him out to Sam a couple of times, when

the going gets tough. She smiles. She sees him too. He gives us comfort.

*

The inquest continues.

Witnesses come and go. The police forensic analyst says that the front brake failed catastrophically, but that the back brake was so badly damaged that he couldn't attribute cause. A bicycle expert that we hired says the bike brakes hadn't been adjusted correctly. The witness who had said that Kadian had been cycling 'like a bat out of hell' withdraws his testimony. He now doesn't think Kadian had been pedalling at the last minute.

Then it is the turn of Richard, the man in the RAF suit. The coroner asks, suspiciously, how he can know that Kadian was travelling at a speed between 25 and 30 mph. He replies that it is his job: he assesses travel speed for Chinook helicopters. He says that Kadian had been 'pumping both brakes', that he had been desperately trying to slow down, that he had been screaming.

And then the bike shop owner takes the stand. He looks anxious, his fingers nervously clutch at the glass of water on the table. Speaking in a low voice that is hard to hear he denies working on the front brake but then assures the coroner that, before he released the bike to Kadian, he had tested both front and back brakes. When our barrister asks him a series of questions, he answers some, but then is told by his lawyer not to answer others.

Finally, at the end of the second day, it is the police accident investigator's turn. He is brief: after extensive research they have ascertained that the collision was caused by one of two things – either Kadian had recklessly ridden out into the road, or his brakes had failed. Having heard the evidence of the past two days, he says, he has determined that it was the second option: both Kadian's front and back brakes had failed.

The coroner appears displeased. As soon as the investigator steps down he calls back the bicycle expert and asks him a series of questions that have the potential to undermine the policeman's statement.

Later, we sit in a cafe in the main square waiting for the coroner to make his decision. I try to remain calm as I tally up the testimony: we have the police investigator's statement, we have the RAF witness whose credibility is beyond doubt, and we have the bicycle shop owner whose statement on the stand appears, at least to us, unreliable.

Two hours after he has adjourned the proceedings, the coroner returns to the court. Once again he explains that this is not a court of blame, and because it is a complex case, he will be declaring a 'narrative verdict'. He then reads it out. It is long. Far longer than I had expected. As he speaks I tap away at my keyboard, recording every word like a stenographer, my emotions held in check by the motion of my fingers.

The coroner starts by saying that he does not believe the government should create further regulations for small businesses. He rejects our request for a system that requires all bicycle mechanics to qualify prior to employment. He rejects the RAF officer's request to have a warning sign put on the path. He says that road signs can actually cause injury, as people might ride into them.

He accepts the bicycle shop owner's statement that he only

worked on the back brake, implying that four witnesses, and Kadian, are liars. He says that he considers my testimony to be unreliable because it is 'tainted by parental bias'.

Finally, he comes to the issue of bicycle failure. He reports that he believes the front brake had experienced a 'catastrophic failure', and as to the back brake . . .

And here my fingers stop typing.

. . . believed that the back brake wasn't working sufficiently as there was no evidence that the bike slowed down or that it skidded.

Waves of relief wash over me. Both brakes had failed.

I look at Deb; she has a small smile on her face.

A few minutes later, the inquest now complete, we climb into the car and drive home, exhausted but vindicated.

*

I receive a text message from my agent. A national newspaper wants me to write a tribute to Kadian.

My first reaction is I'm too tired to do this, I just need a break. But then I realise what a gift this could be, after the brutal intrusion of the coroner and his court.

Each time I speak about Kadian, his life, his death, it gives me a sense of control, release, engagement. Whenever I remain silent, I feel withdrawn, madder, out of control. I know we will be opening ourselves up to further scrutiny – we have not yet begun to recover from the inquest – and from my time as a journalist I know that we will be making ourselves vulnerable by interacting with the national media. Yet it feels right, and, with Debora and Sam's blessing, I write an article of fourteen hundred words.

The editor I am working with is sensitive and compassionate. He even allows me to make last-minute changes well past the deadline as I try to get Kadian's tribute just right.

Around midnight the night before publication I go online to see if the article has been posted yet. It has. I see the headline:

I SAW MY BEAUTIFUL BOY ON THE ROAD. HE WASN'T MOVING.

I am shocked to my core. And angry that the newspaper is doing this to me. To us. I know Deb will be very upset by the headline. I call the news desk and explain my concern, that this article was meant to be a tribute, that the headline is gratuitous, focusing on his death, not the life well lived. The man who takes my call says that he will see what he can do, perhaps the online version could be changed, but it too late for the printed papers which have already been sent to the shops.

In the days that follow I think about my reaction. The sub-editors had simply taken a line from my article, and made it into a headline. Why was I so upset? Certainly, the paper had done nothing wrong.

I realise that seeing the headline was like being told that Kadian was dead, for the very first time. Seeing it was not partial surprise, new information piled on top of old. It was fresh, sudden, startling – as if I knew that he was alive, and then that he was not.

This makes me understand that when people talk about acceptance as being one of the stages of grief they don't have it quite right, at least for me. For me, there are many points of acceptance. Let's say 200, for the sake of argument. By the time I came to write the article I had perhaps experienced twenty such points: seeing Kadian on the road, telling Deb, the ambulance man informing me that he was officially dead, telling Sam, seeing him in the hospital, the death certificate, the burial, and so on. Each one was like being told for the first time. Each one, an instance of revelation, shock and then acceptance. And I realise that I probably have many more of these instances to go, say another 180. I won't fully accept his death until I have endured each one. Perhaps this will never happen.

*

Audrey, the coroner's assistant, sends me an email. I have been chasing her for an answer on the bags inside Kadian's body. It is not clear why she has taken so long to respond. Perhaps she has been trying to protect me. Perhaps they have wanted to hide the truth.

Audrey has spoken to the lab technicians, she writes, and has learned that the bags inside Kadian are not biodegradable.

Even though I have suspected as much, the answer shocks me. They have taken my son from me. They have polluted his body. They have polluted the ground where he lies.

I glance up from the computer screen; tears are running down my face.

*

I worry that I am screwing this up. That I have failed to capture Kadian. That in my desperation to tell a story, I have lost him, that my words have not come close to evoking who he was.

It is so important to get this right. What if, once you have read these words – whether you stop now, or later on, or continue to the very end – you cannot see him? I will have failed him. He who can no longer speak for himself. And if I cannot do it, who will? It is up to me, and this burden fills me with fear.

Should I tell you how I feel about him? How I loved him? Should I provide a list of what made him such an extraordinary person? There are hundreds of words, thousands. If I list these words now, will that do the trick? If I shout them?

Or perhaps silence is best? At Sam's bat mitzvah, eight months after Kadian died, the rabbi gave a sermon in which he spoke about the first letter of the Hebrew alphabet, the aleph, which is silent. It is in silence, he suggested, that we may find Kadian.

Is this true? Can my loud, obnoxious, vibrant son, who spent at least two years of his life bouncing on our bed screaming 'Bob the Builder, can he fix it? Bob the Builder, YES HE CAN!' really be found in silence? How can it when I am deafened by his noise: giggling on the blue rubber mat when I changed his nappies, whooping as he tumbled from the rope swing into the waters of the Antietam Creek on a hot summer's day, laughing and wriggling with joy as I tickled him on the living-room sofa, shouting 'It's muddy, it's muddy' in a northern accent as he cycles through the woods.

Or maybe it would be best to share a story that provides a true, if narrow, glimpse of him, and from that, hope that you can imagine the rest? It might be a good approach: deliverable, measurable.

We are driving somewhere, I can't remember where, I'm not even sure if it's in the US or the UK. It doesn't matter. I am at the wheel, Deb is next to me, Kadian and Sam are behind us. We are on a road trip, we have been in the car for a while, and we still have a way to go. Deb and I are talking – again it doesn't matter about what. What matters is that we are all bored. Kadian has his mother's iPad and starts to record a video of himself. A Joan Armatrading song is playing, she's telling us to 'show some emotion'. At first Kadian just looks into the camera, nodding to the beat, then he crosses his eyes wildly, he puckers his lips like a fish, squeezing them together in time to the beat, then he pushes his tongue in and out of his cheek – first left, then right, then left – then he slowly rotates the iPad 360 degrees, all the time goofing off at the camera, scrunching his eyes, wiggling his nose, all perfectly controlled, all in time to the song. It is a masterclass in visual gaggery, a skit in the spirit of Charlie Chaplin or Mr Bean.

Do you get a sense of him now?

I play this video over and over. It's silly. It's pointless. But I crack up every time I watch it. I hate the fact that this is the closest thing I have to Kadian. But I press play and I watch it again and again.

PART IV

In the summer of 2011 we returned to England.

Kadian was thirteen, Sam was twelve, and both would soon be entering secondary education. If they wanted to attend the top universities then they would have to go to better schools. The local schools were good, but not good enough, we didn't think. We could move out of Shepherdstown, or back to England. I was born in England. My family was there, as were many of our oldest friends, with whom we had stayed in close touch. After ten years in America, we believed that it was time the children experienced their English identity.

And we felt that Kadian had outgrown Shepherdstown. While he hated to leave his friends, and our home, he needed more. As we drove out of town for the last time Kadian said, 'Well, that was a nice little cage to grow up in.'

So we moved back to England. To a small village in Hampshire. It was very different from Shepherdstown. The ladies at the local bakery did not comment on our moods when we purchased bread. Young drunkards wobbled through the streets of the nearby town shouting obscenities. During the winter months our garden was dark by four o'clock. But we appreciated our new home: the startling beauty of the South Downs National Park in which we now lived, the friendliness of our neighbours, the efficient public transport.

Kadian loved to visit London, especially the enormous glass-fronted Apple store in Covent Garden. After his first trip he memorised the route: a car journey to the train station, a one-hour journey to Waterloo, crossing the Thames by the pedestrian bridge, then through the Strand.

In September, Kadian started at Bedales. There was no school uniform and the students called their teachers by their first names. We believed that such informality and individuality would be perfect for Kadian.

Deb took the customary 'first day' photograph, and we walked down to school with him, my arm over his shoulder. I wondered how it would go. Would the kids tease him for his acquired American accent? Would he find it hard to catch up given that the American and English curricula were so different? Would he fit in?

My fears were unfounded. After attending so many schools which hadn't been quite right, here was a place in which the students, teachers and facilities suited Kadian. He blossomed, with a supportive and fun group of friends and terrific reports from his teachers.

He had recently developed Sever's disease – growing pains – that prevented him from doing high-impact sports, so he had spent many afternoons lying on the sports field's grassy banks listening to Adele and Coldplay with one of the other injured students, a girl. Later the mother of this student told us that these lazy afternoons had changed her daughter's life. She was a shy girl, used to hiding behind her long fringe. Following Kadian's attention, she had come out of her shell, and become more outgoing and happy.

*

Sam comes home from Bedales and tells us that she has some big news. She's been speaking to some of Kadian's friends about girls.

We had always wondered about Kadian and romance. When he was younger he had enjoyed dressing up as a princess with Sam and her friends, once even waltzing down the street in a Cinderella dress, his hair pinned back by a tiara, his pink slippers sparkling in the sunlight. It wasn't that we were worried he was gay. We were modern, open-minded parents after all. Then, aged twelve, he had told his mother that he was certain he was straight. This left us curious about one thing: had he ever been kissed?

Sam shares her news. At the end of the previous year, Kadian had been alone with three girls at school. Somehow the subject of kissing had come up and then, whether Kadian had ever been kissed. He told them, sheepishly, that he had not. Apparently, one of the girls had said 'Well, we're going to have to see about that,' stood up, walked over and gave him a good long kiss. Not to be outdone, another of the girls came over and gave Kadian a kiss as well. The third girl, who apparently had a big crush on him, held back, too awkward to join in.

This is another of those bittersweet moments. I am pleased, impressed even, that my son had his first kiss. That it had been two girls at once makes it that much more thrilling. I think it's brilliant that he kept this quiet. But the story comes at a cost. A reminder of all those other moments unconsummated, unenjoyed.

*

As my reason begins to surface, I have started wondering if writing this journal is such a good idea.

When I began it, I just wrote. Sixty thousand words in five weeks. It was more a brain dump than a carefully planned writing exercise. Images and emotions poured out of my mind and onto the computer screen. An unmediated facsimile.

But now, months later, the valve is closing.

After all, what is this? It is becoming less like a journal and more like a biography. Should I really be writing a biography of Kadian?

How does one write a biography of a fourteen-year-old boy? His life not yet lived. His major accomplishments not yet accomplished. Is it possible to be objective when I am part of the story? Perhaps objectivity is the last thing I should seek. More than this, is it too soon to be writing? Or is this the best time to write, trapped as I am in the white heat of grief?

And what about privacy? Kadian never agreed to this.

I have shared this text with Deb and Sam, who have agreed that others can see it. But these words are mine, I must take responsibility for them. This scares me. It would be terrible if I failed, if they or others were to be disappointed or offended by my attempt.

I also worry that I am in danger of presenting an airbrushed version of my son. But is it not the purpose of the eulogiser to shed only positive light on the eulogee? Is it not bad form to find fault with the dead? After all, they are no longer here to defend themselves.

If someone was going to write a biography of me, what would they say? Would they only focus on my accomplishments, or would they also, if they were honest, reveal some of the uglier episodes, those I would really not like anyone to know about. The time I threw a cat at my friend, Harry, when I was twelve years old (he never spoke to me again). The day I stole ten pence from my mother's purse so I could buy a Mars bar (which I had been forbidden to eat the previous day). The afternoon my son rode his bike down a hill, and was hit by a van, when I was in charge, and should have stopped him.

And of Kadian, what can I say that makes him look bad? Sometimes, he would claim his sister had bullied him, when he himself had instigated the fighting. Sometimes he would sneak into the kitchen, or the pantry, or to wherever the chocolate bars, cookies, cakes were stored, and eat another. The apple, apparently, did not fall far from the sugar tree. While he often worked extremely hard, there were times when he was lazy, because he did not see a need to be otherwise. But is this fair, to chronicle his faults when he had not lived long enough to experiment, let alone see or understand the consequence of his inaction?

When it is known that a politician was caught smoking an illegal substance at sixteen, or eighteen, or twenty-one, they are given a pass. 'He was young,' people say, 'he was experimenting. That is what he was meant to do.' But what if a biography was written of Barack Obama, say, at the age of fourteen? Would we judge him harshly, would we hold him accountable for his misdeeds? To what standard should a biographer hold his young subject? To what standard should I hold Kadian?

I struggle with these questions.

*

June 2013

It has been an intense year for Sam. Not only has she lost her brother, but it has been her first year at Bedales. Navigating her way around the school, meeting classmates, coping with schoolwork and a new set of teachers.

A few weeks into her first term she described having to attend school so soon after her brother's death as 'morally wrong', but what choice did she have? To miss a year of school would have tripped her up down the road. All the while the pain has remained close to the surface, and although we have spent days on the sofa, unable to function in any normal way, she has exhibited extraordinary fortitude.

We speak frequently to her teachers to monitor her progress, to ensure that she is taken care of, that she is protected from careless remarks and sensitive subjects. Sometimes it is impossible to avoid triggers. In one lesson she is asked to write a paragraph about her brother. In another she is told to write an essay about attending the funeral of a loved one in ancient Greece. In this last assignment she writes that she cannot understand why people would want a life after death if they would have to see the heartbreak of their loved ones down on Earth.

And the school continues to remember Kadian. He is

mentioned during assembly, the school organises a trip to his burial site for his friends, a picture of Kadian hangs in the school sanctuary. Many of the students, particularly Sam's friends, wear the purple 'Kadian' bracelets that were handed out at the memorial service. He is not going to be forgotten. Her loss is not going to be forgotten.

Sam appears to be doing well. Somehow, and maybe it is due to her elastic teenage brain, she is able to feel the pain *and* thrive at her new school. She is more able to socialise, better able to travel, and less fearful of outside stimulus and conflict than us. She is hungrier for life, and for tomorrow.

But there are moments of profound grief, usually taken quietly, alone and in her bedroom. On her terms, in her own time.

It is now the start of the summer holidays. We are sitting in our living room on separate sofas. Cups of tea in our hands. We are a few weeks away from the first-year anniversary of Kadian's death and we aren't sure what to do.

Sam has been invited to go to Canada for two weeks with a friend of hers. It means that she will be away for the anniversary. We ask her what she wants, sensitive that she should make her own mind up. 'I want to go to Canada,' she says. 'I don't want to leave you two, but I also don't want to miss out on this opportunity.'

At first we all agree that she should go. Sam says, 'Are you sure you are OK with me going?' I realise that I am not. This isn't right, I tell them. We need to be together for this anniversary, especially as it will be the first. We are creating new rituals, habits that will probably be repeated for the rest of our lives. Surely, on this day, even if not others, we should always strive to be together, even if it means flying across the world.

They smile. Deb is thankful that I have articulated what she has been thinking. Sam is thankful that we are taking command, being the parents that she needs us to be. And I am thankful that I have something to look forward to, something to get up in the morning for. I have someone that I need to look after.

I am holding on to that thread.

*

Things grew tense between Kadian and me after we moved back to England. I found myself correcting him for the smallest of things: for the way he held his fork, for not taking out the rubbish, for not putting away his clean clothes.

He began to spend more time playing video games, something that, unlike most of his friends, he had never done before. For hours he pecked away at his laptop, constructing buildings on some alien world.

As soon as he came home from school he sat in the Internet cafe – the name we gave to the dining room of our house, which we had filled with sofas, small tables and computers – and, without so much as a 'How was your day?' or 'Nice to see you', he logged on to his game.

I told him once that his behaviour was not acceptable, that common courtesies were important, and he stormed out of the room, and up to his bedroom to continue the game. 'At least he was downstairs with us,' said Debora, annoyed that I had been so harsh.

I was turning into some authoritarian, angry, irrational

father figure, but I couldn't stop myself. It was as if, despite all my resolutions, we were hard-wired to be at each other's throats.

A distance began to form between us. A coldness. I couldn't reach him. Now whenever I corrected him for some minor misdeed, he would just say, sarcastically, 'I am a bad person,' and walk off. When I asked him why he hadn't performed a chore he would simply answer, 'I am lazy.'

I was harder on him than I was on Sam. If she hadn't emptied the dishwasher, I would remind her, gently, and then again, and again, never losing my temper. Not so with Kadian. As soon as he failed in some small way, I was immediately on his case, harsh, sharp, unforgiving. He told me to stop 'yelling' at him. I said I hadn't raised my voice, and was merely being firm. He said 'yelling' referred to a tone of voice, not volume. I said this wasn't true in England. He said this was true in America. He was right, I was being too harsh. But again, I couldn't stop myself. It had become a character issue: Kadian the insolent, disobedient son, Thomas the overbearing, quick-to-temper father.

The family split into two camps. Me and Sam, Deb and Kadian. On walks, Kadian dropped back to spend time with his mother, who walked at a slower pace, Sam and I trailblazing ahead. We shopped as pairs. Watched movies in pairs. It was not always like this, but the trend was emerging, and we were all aware of it. Sometimes the subject came up, but it was difficult to talk about, we became tetchy. Sometimes we would joke about it, the Mum/Kadian team, the Dad/Sam team.

Then Deb started travelling once a month to the USA on

business and Kadian withdrew further still. He came down for dinner, but complained that he didn't like my cooking. I had burned the sausages again, or the potatoes were overcooked. I had a go at him for not finishing the food on his plate. After dinner, he retreated to his bedroom, taking a phone with him. Through the door I heard his voice. He was talking with his mother. It appeared to be a long conversation.

*

I have been thinking about the moment when Sam will become older than Kadian. When I cannot sleep at night, I calculate their age difference, the time left.

I even create a spreadsheet adding and subtracting the precise hour (based on their different birth dates and Kadian's time of death) when Sam will overtake Kadian. I worry that the moment will mark some seismic shift, and I fixate on the date while trying my hardest not to think about it.

Then, as the moment approaches, I come to realise that Kadian was, is, older than Sam. He will always be her big brother. I stop counting out the days.

*

I take a train to London, and then get on the Underground to Hammersmith to meet my cousin, James. He has been a rock throughout the last year. Despite his extraordinarily busy life, he has called me almost every day, visited us at home regularly, and even had groceries delivered to our door.

As I rumble through London, I observe that travelling has become less problematic. I am less startled by the jerking movement of the carriages, the crush of bodies, the flickering lights as the train passes through a tunnel. Maybe my PTSD symptoms are diminishing.

Once at James's house, we decide to go for a walk with his two-year-old son, Samuel, to see the ducks in the park. Samuel runs off across the lawns. 'You're so fast!' James shouts. Willing myself to join the game, I run after the little boy, huffing as I pretend that he outpaces me. 'Samuel, you're so fast!' I repeat.

We reach a large pond. 'Let's feed the ducks,' says Samuel. James hands him a wad of stale bread. My mind drifts off, to Kadian. I will myself to be present. 'Look,' I say, 'there's a swan, Samuel. Can you throw him some too?' Tearing off a few crumbs, he throws them to the swan, who greedily dabs his beak into the water.

We come to a small grassy hill. 'You want to roly-poly?' asks James. Samuel nods excitedly and together they walk up the slope. Samuel lies down at the top and then, sausage-like and already giggling, rolls down.

'You want to have a turn?' James asks me gently. I take Samuel's hand and we walk back up the hill. Down we come. I am rolling as well, arms out straight above my head, ankles spinning, laughing freely.

Back at their house, we eat tea and cake, and I lie on a sofa, with Samuel on my chest. He falls asleep. It feels so good, his warm body on my mine, solid. This is what I miss the most, this contact. It is not about memories recalled or emotions triggered.

This is something entirely physical. It is like a thirst I cannot quench, a hankering I cannot satisfy. But I put aside the inevitable pain, and with Samuel's warm head on my chest, I drift off too.

*

Deb was away in the US again, and at home things had spiralled out of control.

The kids were fighting, as siblings do. One pushed the other, one was hurt. As usual, I blamed Kadian. He said I wasn't being fair, but I refused to listen. He shouted at the injustice, and I lost my head, and grabbed his arm, too hard, forcing him to sit on the sofa. He ran upstairs to his bedroom and tried to call his mother, but couldn't reach her. He called Charlie, our close friend, instead.

I tried to call Deb too, and got through. I explained to her what had happened. Unusually for me in in such conversations, I was not defensive. I told her that I was not doing my job properly, I was frustrated at the distance between me and Kadian, and said that I needed help. She listened, calmly and without judgement, and suggested that I tell Kadian what I had just told her.

It was midnight by now, and in my white terry-cloth dressing gown, I padded down the corridor to Kadian's room. His light was off but I knew he was still awake. 'Kadian,' I said quietly, careful not to wake Sam who was asleep in the next room, 'can I come in?'

'Sure' he said softly. I could tell by the rasp in his voice that he had been crying.

I sat down on the floor, back against the warm radiator, my knees drawn up against my chest.

And we talked. I apologised, sharing my fears as a father with him, that I wanted to be the best I could be, that I knew I hadn't been doing a good job, that I had not being treating him fairly or with enough respect. He apologised for being cross with me, for not listening, for raising his voice. Soon we were both crying. After thirty minutes or so, I suggested that maybe it was time for sleep. He agreed, I stood up, walked over to him, kissed him on his warm forehead. He held me close, tight, I tried to pull away, but he didn't release me, so I relaxed, lingered a little longer. 'Goodnight, Kads,' I said.

'Best father in the world,' he said.

'Best son in the world,' I replied.

*

The Sustainability Centre's campsite is empty when we pull up. A ghost town of tepees, yurts and solar-powered showers.

It is almost a year since Kadian died and Deb, Sam and I have decided to take over the campsite for a weekend. A few weeks back we sent an email to our close family and friends inviting them to join us. We expect them to be arriving soon.

Deb has visited often over the past twelve months. I have come less frequently. This is the first time that we have returned as a group since Kadian's burial.

The campsite is located on a small grassy field surrounded by woods. We have the place to ourselves and can fill it with as much noise and activity as we want. It's a perfect way to remember and celebrate Kadian. He loved to camp, he loved being with friends and family, and he will be close by.

It is four in the afternoon. There is a lot to do. We unpack the car: tents, sleeping bags, cookware, wood, a massive stainless-steel gas-powered barbecue, chairs, a giant orange plastic water cooler, and enough food to keep thirty people happy for two days.

My sister Amanda and her kids are the next to arrive, driving all the way from France. After that come Cat, Gillian and Gary, who have flown in from New York. The rest pitch up in twos, threes and fours. By the time the tents are erected, the tepees and yurts assigned and occupied, and the sleeping bags are laid out, the sun is setting over the thick band of trees next to the campsite.

I am in the makeshift kitchen, grilling burgers and sausages, pouring drinks, grating cheese and handing out plates. If I just stay busy enough, I think to myself, fill the time with chores and easy interactions, perhaps I can get through it.

Later, we gather around an open fire, logs piled high, flames crackling towards the clear star-filled sky, some sitting on blankets, others on collapsible chairs, a bottle of whisky passing from one adult to the next, as owls hoot from the trees. We share stories about Kadian, moments of joy flickering in the firelight.

*

A few days after my midnight chat to Kadian, I woke up to find pink sticky notes pasted all over the house – on the bathroom mirror, the inside of my clothes cupboard, attached to the coffee maker, on my computer screen – upon which were written the words 'You are so cheeky!'

Kadian was back to teasing me. Back to challenging me, but in a funny way.

We were close again.

*

The next day, after breakfast, a giant game of baseball begins. Next to a diamond of discarded sweaters, the group separates into teams, picked by two of the youngest children. Normally, I would have been a gleeful participant, eager to be at the centre of such family fun. Instead, I hang back in the kitchen area clearing up the breakfast things. Each time the ball is batted a peal of delight and encouragement rings out and I recoil. Kadian's absence is too present. I cannot be part of it. I don't want to spoil the fun.

Once the game is finished, we have lunch, and then we walk as a group down to Kadian's site. This time I am at the front, pushing a two-metre-high, half-a-metre-wide, roughly cut wooden stool on a metal cart. The stool has been carved from a single trunk by our friend Andy – an excellent carpenter. The back of the stool has been carved into the shape of a wizard's cloak. Kadian's name is engraved on the top edge of the stool's back, and carved on the inside are words from Sam's song 'Beautiful Boy': 'I will be with you everywhere'.

The journey through the woods to Kadian's site is less dream-like than it had been during his burial. I stop a few times, partly to adjust the orange straps that hold the stool tight to the cart, but also to remind myself that I can, that the world around me is, to a degree, within my control. That I am not merely a spectator.

At his site, we unwrap the stool from the cart and heave it to the head of Kadian's grave. It quickly finds its spot, level and sturdy. Different people try it out, children first, then the adults, enjoying the comfort and the view.

With the stool now in place the group is quiet. As with the burial, no words are spoken. This time, there are no rose petals on the ground, no leaves to throw in the grave, no Beethoven's 9th playing on a portable speaker.

Instead, we stand together, an unbroken ring, holding each other up. Acknowledging that even though twelve months have gone by, our loss has not diminished, our pain has not lessened. It is a commitment that we will continue to support each other in our love for Kadian.

And while we gather amid the birch and the hazel, around the grave of my teenage son, I utter a silent thanks for these kind, strong people, without whose support I would not have been able to survive.

*

Ever since he was small Kadian had loved to climb. Lamp posts, trees, fences. One day Deb and Kadian went shopping to Ikea. Deb turned around in the car park and when she turned back Kadian wasn't there. She couldn't find him. Then she heard a noise and looked up – he was thirty feet off the ground, legs wrapped around a skinny grey pole, an Ikea flag fluttering above him. It brought him joy to torment his mother, who was forever fearful – 'I can't look', she would say – by climbing to the very top of a tree, laughing as he swayed with the wind.

That didn't mean he was blind to risk. Far from it. He had a great fear of roads, greater than anyone I had ever met. Until he was ten or so he wasn't permitted to cross any roads without an adult. When he got a little older he was allowed to cross the small roads near our house, but couldn't wander further afield until he had repeatedly proved himself, passing a series of trials no less stringent than a driving test.

His fear of crossing roads bubbled up again when we moved to England. We had just finished a three-hour walk – Kadian, Sam and myself – across muddy fields and through damp woods. We were all tired and ready for the hike's end. Skirting by a golf course, we found the footpath had deposited us at the edge of a four-lane dual carriageway with no clear way to get across. On the other side we could see a footpath sign.

'Let's wait till there's a gap, then we can hurry over,' I said. Sam nodded, all business, focused on the cars, calculating how much time we would need, how much of a gap we should wait for.

Kadian backed away. 'I don't think this is a good idea,' he said. 'Can't we find another way?' The colour had drained from his face. 'It'll be safe enough, Kads,' I said. 'We'll just have to wait a while to make sure we have plenty of time.'

'But what if one of us trips, or a car comes too fast?' he said.

'We'll be fine,' I answered.

Normally some reassurance would work. But not today. He backed away even further; he was now a good fifteen feet from the road's edge, and looked to be close to a panic attack.

I glanced at Sam. She shrugged. 'OK,' I said, a little too late, a little too disappointed. 'Let's find another way.' We walked a few yards down the road and almost immediately spotted an underpass. He had been absolutely right, it would have been foolish to have attempted the crossing. I felt guilty that I had encouraged my children to take the risk, to trust in what was a very poor decision. Luckily, I hadn't insisted. Luckily, I had listened to Kadian.

Each of these words, each of these stories, now resounds with deeper meanings. The 'what ifs' and the 'could haves' and the 'if onlys' pile up and pile up and pile up.

Not yet, not yet. I am not quite ready to go there.

*

Kadian and a few of his Bedales school friends decided to build their own server. They wanted to control the parallel universe they were constructing in their video game, Kadian explained. Not only would it make the game faster, but it would also protect them from unwanted players. They'd already pooled their pocket money and purchased some memory cards for the task. Kadian asked if he could have my old PCs. I was still anxious about the amount of time Kadian was spending on the computer, but wanting to be supportive, and mindful of our recent fight, I said yes.

Kadian had come up with the idea. They would establish a company, he said, with each of the boys providing funds and acting as shareholders. The shareholders would dictate the direction of the project, and decide who would act as the server's administrators. After some discussion, it was agreed that all the founding members would be administrators.

Over the next few weeks they gathered in our house on Wednesday afternoons, and on an old 1950s Diner oval table that stood by our living-room window, they took apart the PCs. Fans, memory cards and graphic boards were carefully prised out and placed in a plastic box, ready for use.

One of the boys who'd joined the project, let's call him Josh, quickly established himself as the brains of the operation, instructing the others, and describing each component and its potential worth. For much of the time, Kadian sat on the arm of the sofa, cross-legged, watching. He was less certain when it came to non-Apple computers.

Before long the server was up and running, and Kadian was back in his room, tapping away at his video game. 'Look, Dad! It works!' I peered over. He was building a complicated orange-brick edifice. 'We had to start again,' he laughed. 'Last night one of the others created a wild beast which knocked the buildings down.' I murmured something non-committal. I still couldn't see the point to it.

The next day Kadian was quiet when he returned home from school. He didn't talk during dinner, he played with his food, and went to bed without saying goodnight. Deb went up to find out what was wrong. It took her some time, but she finally teased it out of him. Kadian was upset that Josh had granted himself administrative rights even though he wasn't a shareholder. Josh didn't like being criticised, and locked Kadian out of the server. Uncomfortable with the conflict, his friends told him to drop it but, for Kadian, it was too much to take. He quit.

The next few days were rough. He was short-tempered with his sister, and curt with his mother and me. But by the weekend, the cloud had lifted. I asked him what had changed, and he told me that he'd decided it was all for the best. He had been spending too much time playing video games and wanted to do something else. He said that the others had apologised for locking him out, and had left the project too. They had talked about other activities, away from their computer screens. One of their ideas was to go out for bike rides in the countryside.

*

I open Facebook and type. 'Where the fuck is he?'

The words hover on the page, unposted. Should I share this? I want them to know, it is an aggressive, unsubtle act. I don't care about the consequences. I click on the 'post' button.

Then I delete it. Why should others see it? Why ruin their day? But I want to. I want to ruin their day. So I type it again, and post it.

'Where the fuck is he?' This time I leave it.

*

9 July 2012

Kadian was sitting on the living-room floor, cross-legged, one foot sitting on a thigh, lotus-like, a huge smile on his face. He was unpacking his new bicycle.

This was a Christmas-morning moment for him. Not only was he getting his dream bike, he was going to build it himself.

He carefully removed the contents of the box, the wheels, the seat stem, the pedals, the frame.

It was the culmination of the long, six-month obsession, kick-started by Gin, in Washington DC. He knew he wanted to build a bike, but what kind of bike? Should it be made of aluminium or steel? Should the angle between the top tube and seat tube be sharp, making it an exciting, responsive ride, or shallow, providing comfort and stability? Should he get a 50-inch frame, to fit him perfectly, or a 52-inch frame, which he could grow into? After all, this would be the bike that would carry him into adulthood, and maybe beyond. Should he build up a bike from scratch, purchasing each part separately, or should he buy a ready-to-build bike, and upgrade the parts as he went along?

Deb had just booked a family holiday to the Pyrenees for later that summer – a chance for Kadian to improve his Spanish, but also a perfect place for long bike rides. A touring bike would be ideal for the trip: something that would be forgiving over long distances, and could easily withstand the bumps of the road.

At last, he decided on a matt-black 50-inch Surly Long Haul Trucker, the king of touring bikes, with double-butted Reynolds 531 aluminium tubing, Shimano components and Mavic wheels. He decided to upgrade the brakes immediately, so that both brakes and gears could be operated from the same handlebar levers.

The choice of saddle proved more difficult. Should he stick to a conventional, soft, padded touring seat, or buy a Brooks saddle, the same saddle I had used when I travelled around the world, but which required a lot of looking after, and a long time to break in? Eventually, he calculated that the Brooks was beyond his reach. Maybe it could be a birthday present, he told us.

*

I am so angry. I have never been this angry before. Deb and I are fighting. She shouts that I am not listening to her. I shout that she isn't being reasonable. I can't remember what the argument is about.

Normally, I would have stopped myself, taken a few deep breaths. But the thought of this reminds me of Kadian. Whenever he was upset, or frustrated, or enraged, he would try and control his emotions by breathing deeply, but often to the extent that he hyperventilated, causing him to panic, which made him even worse.

'I have had it!' I shout. I long to rage, I am hungry for it. Deb looks at me in surprise. I stride out of the living room, almost at a run, and scream. A five-second scream. It feels so good. I stop, look up and see the white of the hallway wall. I punch it as hard as I can. Fuck that hurts. There is a small dent. I want the hole to be bigger. I punch it again. No mark. I remember that this wall is not made of soft plasterboard, but concrete. That's why it hurts so much.

The failure makes me angrier still. I scream again and grab a chair, throwing it behind me. It strikes a mannequin that Deb has spent the past few weeks covering with buttons. I should feel guilty, I realise, but I don't. Screaming again I stomp upstairs. From the living room I hear Deb shout, 'I will not live like this! I will not put up with this abuse!'

I pace my bedroom like a wild animal in a cage, filled with adrenalin and rage. I cast my eyes around for my next target, and then, suddenly, it is gone. The anger dissipates, I feel embarrassed and alone. I just want to get out. I quickly run downstairs, grab a jumper, hat and jacket from the coatstand in the hallway, and slip outside, quietly shutting the door behind me.

It is dark outside. And very cold. I walk to the left, and left again, along a narrow country road that leads towards the hills behind our house. Shivering, I wrap my jacket around me, and look up at the sky. It is filled with stars, as clear as it was the night that Kadian died and Sam, James and I lay on the lawn of my parents' garden in Wiltshire.

I am overcome, without energy or impulse. Falling to my knees, my palms pressed against the cold black tarmac as if in prayer, I wail and wail and wail. I am lost, alone, naked in my grief. The pain is unbearable.

*

He was spending hours by himself in his room again. But this time he was building his bike.

Every few hours I popped in to see how things were coming along, congratulating him on his progress, sharing in his excitement about some new discovery.

'Did you know you can adjust the gears if you turn this screw?' he said, or 'Did you know that you should inflate your tyres to different pressures depending on the road surface?'

The bike frame was suspended from a tall red stand that leaned against his bedroom wall. When he wasn't sure what to do next, he asked me for help, or called one of the mechanics working at Deb's bike shop. And just about every tip he could possibly need was on YouTube, or in one of the bike mechanics' chat rooms he found online. Always a problem-solver, this bike assembly was just another puzzle for him to complete. Soon he was adding the wheels, the pedals and the seat. It began to look like a proper bike. Like the one I had spent a year on when I was eighteen years old. I was very aware of the pattern; I was glad of it.

Once the bike was assembled and had been checked by a local bike shop, Kadian took it for a short test ride in the lane behind the house. Soon he and a school friend were spending every day on their bikes, visiting local lakes, bringing back shopping from the supermarket, touring the nearby villages. They were independent, adventurous, carefree. Two boys on their bikes with time on their hands, what could be better?

*

On the street outside our house I bump into Dinah, one of our neighbours. She gives me a hug. 'I'm so glad to see you,' she says, her voice muffled in my shoulder. 'We've been thinking about you so much. How are you?' I begin to share one of my scripted responses, but she stops me. 'You need to know,' she says, looking me in the eye, 'this could have happened to any of us. It happened to you, but we're doing this together, we're sharing your pain.'

A couple of weeks later, I have lunch with Jez, an old friend of mine. We are sitting at a small table next to a lake in St James's Park. We catch up with each other's lives. Soon we are talking about Kadian. Jez says, 'You know, what you're experiencing is every parent's worst nightmare. It's something I think about every time my kids climb a tree, swing on a rope, swim in the sea.'

I think about this and realise that I too had these feelings. The everyday near-misses: when he jumped across a river and slipped just before take-off; when he launched down a steep Alpine piste, fell, and slid down the slope on his front; when he was cycling along a country road near our house and had to dive into a hedgerow to avoid being hit by a Land Rover.

'You now have a task,' Jez says, cutting into my thoughts. 'You have to share your experiences, you have to tell the rest of us how awful it is, how terrible. That's what you now have to do.'

A few days later I meet my cousin James for a walk along the Thames in Hammersmith. It is the middle of the afternoon, the path is empty, the air is cold, a few seagulls peck at the gravelly sand at the river's edge.

He asks me how my therapy sessions are going. I give an uncertain response, and he bombards me with questions: 'How often are you seeing him? Is he helping? Is he the right person?'

At first, I am inclined to accept his concern. I'm not seeing him enough. Yes he's helping. Yes he's the right person. Then I stop walking, turn and face him.

'You know, you have been absolutely amazing these past months,' I start slowly, anxious that I fully convey my appreciation for his love and support. Anxious that I might do anything that could change things between us, at this time when I need him the most. 'I know you hate seeing me like this. But I need you to accept it, to carry the burden of it, all this shit, all this pain. My son is dead. There is no cure.'

He is quiet for a moment, and looks pained. 'I'm so sorry,' he says. 'Of course, I totally understand what you're saying.'

He pauses. 'Does that mean I have to be sad too?' One of his great gifts is that he is able to make me laugh, even at the most difficult of times. We laugh, and continue on.

*

11 July 2012

Kadian and I set out for a walk to the Poet's Stone. As we strolled down the lane I looked at him. He was a man now. His face had narrowed, his chin had become thickset, his cheekbones more pronounced. Now bulked up from exercise, his arms were strong, capable of holding me down on the floor when we wrestled. Unlike mine, his legs were long and thin making him almost my height. Indeed, he had started hugging me from behind, arms around my waist, head on my shoulders. In a few months I knew that he would be taller than me.

It was a gorgeous, blue-sky day. The paths up the steep hill – which were so wet and slippery in the winter – were now dry and dusty, beaded with streaks of silvery chalk. We climbed the hill without pause, both fit and energetic.

At the top, we sat on the bench overlooking the valley and talked about his time at Bedales. He had just completed his first year. He told me that it had been wonderful, the best year of his life. He loved his friends, his teachers were interesting, supportive and friendly, he couldn't wait to go back at the end of the summer.

Mindful that this might upset him, I asked him what he thought about his grades. According to his teachers his grades were good but not as good as they could be. Rather than react to my fatherly intrusion or my tone, that in former days he might have taken as disappointment or, worse, micro-management, he said that he was not happy with his results and that he intended to do better next year. 'You don't have to worry', he said, 'this was meant to be a fun year. The chance to get to know the people in my class. The hard work starts next term.'

We gazed at the glorious view of the valley below. 'So how's the book going?' he asked. *Hanns and Rudolf* had been six years in the making, and Kadian knew that I had struggled while writing it. There were times when I had been close to giving up. I told him that my first meeting with my publishers had gone very well. Towards the end of the process I had become so sick of the manuscript that I'd taken to reading portions of it to Kadian and Sam, until they too had tired of it. 'Stop talking to us about Nazis,' they had frequently told me.

'You know,' said Kadian, smiling in his cheeky way, 'I can now tell my friends that you're an author. Up till now I didn't know what to tell them, a lay-about perhaps, a house husband.' And then his tone grew serious and he looked me directly in the eye. 'I want you to know, I'm so proud of you, Dad. I'm so pleased that after all your hard work your book is going to be published.'

We sat in silence, as the sun started to set over the valley. Then Duke began whining. He wanted to resume our walk. I threw him a stick, wanting to delay our departure for just a short while longer. Then, when the time seemed right, I said, 'Shall we go?' With a nod from Kadian, we stood, and with my arm around his shoulder, we began our descent.

*

The sun slices through my office window, illuminating a thousand shimmering dust particles in the air. My eyes track one particular strand of fluff as it falls slowly to the floor. Then I lose focus, my mind suddenly captured by sorrow.

A new thought pops into my mind. The dust is always there, floating. But it is only when the sun shines at a particular angle, when there are no clouds to block its path, when I am sitting in a certain position, that I can see the particles floating, spinning, falling, rising. Is this how it will be with Kadian, with my memories?

When people ask me how I feel, I tell them it is like I am sitting in an enormous, cavernous theatre. The lights are on in one small part of the auditorium, in the section where I am sitting. The stage is dark, as are the upper levels, the balconies, the foyer, the car park, the dressing rooms and the basement. I can sit still, I can talk to others who walk into my section, but I see and hear nothing else. All is darkness.

And when they ask, my friends, 'Have these symptoms got better?' I say to them that they have. The lights are beginning to come on in the circle and on the stage. I can see more of the auditorium, the aisles, the seats around me. It is getting lighter.

Yet I still suffer from post-traumatic shock. Some days I feel light-headed, a buzzing in the brain, a racing heart and a sense of panic gripping my body. Such days are spent on the sofa, watching old television series on the Internet, making breakfast, making lunch, making dinner. Lacking focus, crushed by lethargy and depression, unable to work. All I can do is wait for my energy to return.

Time continues to play tricks with my head. It feels as though I am trapped in that day, on 25 July 2012, or perhaps it is better to say that that day has not ended, I never made it to 26 July.

The rigid edges of time have softened. I live both in that moment and in no moment. The calendar says that Kadian died twelve months ago; to me it feels like fifteen minutes.

Sometimes, just as I look elsewhere, away from Kadian, he comes crashing back, without warning. When we sit at a table in a restaurant with four place settings, and the waiter, seeing that there are only three of us, removes the extra cutlery.

Or when people ask, 'Do you have children?' and I am faced with either denying his existence, which is awful, or telling them that my fourteen-year-old son was killed in a bike accident, which either stops the conversation, leaving only silence, or triggers a series of intrusive questions (How did he die? Were you there? How have you been?)

In other moments, when Kadian has drifted away for too long, I rush to bring him back. I might say, 'Kadian would have liked that' or 'Do you remember when Kadian . . .?' Any story that involves him, a moment that we all shared.

And I wonder, how am I going to finish this journal? How can I stop writing about his life? I want it to be perfect – anything else would dishonour his memory. And there is so much more to say, so many stories to choose from. I want to share everything, but to do so would take fourteen years. What moments should I choose? What moments make a man? A life?

Worse, the idea of stopping reminds me too much of his death. I want to stay close to him. I don't want to leave him. From writing this journal I have become even more grateful for the fourteen and a half years that we had together. Above all, this is what I want to focus on, not Kadian's death, but Kadian as he was, alive.

I don't want to turn the page. But then I tell myself that this journal is just a part of the remembering, it is not the whole. I shouldn't fear it ending.

*

14 July 2012

It was an ordinary day, just like any other.

Kadian was fourteen and a half. Sam was thirteen and a half. We were all together at home in England.

Kadian slept in. Eventually he wandered downstairs, wearing a pair of jeans with a fraying hole in each knee and his blue City Bikes T-shirt, the word 'staff' printed across his chest. Sam woke up a few minutes later and joined us in the kitchen. She was wearing her pink Mickey Mouse pyjamas.

We ate breakfast together. Kadian had bread, butter and marmalade. Sam had bread and Nutella. Deb and I ate muesli. Sam and I drank cups of Tetley tea with milk. Kadian and Deb drank lattes. We didn't talk much. Kadian read the writing on the back of the cereal pack. Sam stared into space. I read the *New Yorker*. Deb texted someone on her iPhone.

Across the table I noticed that Kadian had a piece of marmalade rind stuck on his top lip. 'You are the world's messiest eater,' I said. He reached up, wiped his lip and continued reading the cereal box.

The kids put their plates in the dishwasher, then headed into the living room. Sam sat on the plump black armchair and switched on the TV. Kadian opened his laptop and began watching Apple videos on YouTube.

I cleaned up the kitchen, then I joined them, changing the channel to an American Football game. Deb sat at the piano, playing Chopin, then Elton John, then Beethoven. Duke was asleep on his bed in the corner.

A couple of hours later, one of us suggested we take him for a walk. It was raining again. Kadian pulled on his scuffed-up brown Blundstone work boots, his grey woollen pea coat and his Union Jack hat. The rest of us wore wellies and rain jackets. We walked down the road, past the waterfall, along the muddy track and up the hill to the Poet's Stone. We talked about nothing in particular – the weather, the condition of the track, the week we'd had. At the top we gazed at the view, paused for a few moments, then returned home.

That night, we made dinner. Spaghetti and pesto. Kadian told us his latest joke. Sam sang a silly ditty she'd made up. Deb had to go to the US for her next work trip soon. We talked about what train she would catch, what food we needed to order from the supermarket, what bills needed to be paid.

After dinner we returned to the living room. We watched TV: *Glee* and then *Downton Abbey*. None of us particularly enjoyed them, but it didn't matter.

At nine, Sam said she was ready for bed. Kissing us goodnight she walked upstairs. At eleven or so, Deb and I followed her up, telling Kadian to go to bed soon, reminding him to let the dog out and turn off the lights. A few minutes later we heard the sound of running water from his bathroom. He was going to take one of his late-night baths.

Half an hour later he walked into our room dressed in his pyjamas. He dived onto the blankets that covered our bed. I noticed how long his legs were.

'Goodnight, Dad,' he said, giving me his special kiss – his

lips to my forehead, chin, left cheek, right cheek, and then his nose brushing mine.

'Love you,' I said.

'Goodnight, Mum,' he said, turning to Deb, and giving her the same kiss.

'Love you,' she said.

He clambered up, and I shouted, 'Close the door!'

*

It is one in the morning. I cannot sleep. Acid fills my stomach.

I get out of bed and quietly walk downstairs. Turning on the light, I grab my computer and sit on the sofa.

On Facebook I see that Charlie is online. I send him a message.

'I can't sleep,' I say, 'I am struggling with the guilt.'

I have talked to Charlie before about how I am feeling. There is no need to explain.

An icon appears. I can see that he is writing.

'I feel guilty I wasn't there to help him with his bike.' A pause. 'We can all find reasons to feel guilty if we're looking for them.'

'But I should have done more,' I reply.

'Of course this is going to drive you crazy now. But from everything I heard about this, you were very focused on making sure the bike was safe.'

'But I led the ride. I was the father. I was responsible.'

'Hindsight is 20/20 – there are so many things we know now because we have connected the dots. Bike shops are the experts we trust to make the bike safe. He took it to two of them.'

'Yes.'

I wait while he writes his next message. The icon appears.

'Do you remember the movie *Fearless*,' he writes, 'with Rosie Perez. She lost her baby in a plane crash when it flew out of her arms. She is plagued by guilt – thinking that if she had just been able to hold on she could have saved the baby. It might be worth a viewing. Great movie. Jeff Bridges helps her understand – in a very unconventional way.'

He sends me a link to a web-page. It is a clip from the movie. I watch it. To help the Rosie character, Jeff Bridges puts her in his car, places a fire extinguisher in her arms, and, having made sure that they are both buckled up, drives into a brick wall. The extinguisher flies out of Rosie's arms, but she is fine. She understands that she could not have held on to the baby and that therefore it is not her fault.

I message him back. 'So what is the point here?'

'The idea that you would have done anything consciously to put Kadian in danger is just absurd. I have seen you over the years being relentlessly protective of Kadian in every respect. If you could have done anything to save Kadian, you would have done so without thinking about it. So this guilt thing is just a misfiring of your brain.'

'What you're saying is I could not have saved him.'

'I don't think so – not unless you had some kind of X-ray bike mechanic vision. You told him to fix the brakes and he took them to be fixed. They looked like they worked.'

'Yes they did.'

'If you knew what you do now, you might do things differently – but how could you know all those things?'

'Of course, if I knew the brakes weren't working, we wouldn't have gone on the ride.'

'Exactly.'

I have run out of steam. It is late. I tell Charlie I have to go to bed. He says goodnight.

Back in bed I close my eyes.

I am still in the well but I am climbing now. The walls are wet and slippery, I scrape my knees and elbows on the sharp craggy edges, but I am climbing. I know which direction I am going in. Up.

*

17 July 2012

When he was small, Kadian had travelled to Indianapolis to visit his cousin Taylor. Taylor had a tree house, built by his grandfather – a shingle-roofed hut with pulley, rope and bucket that sat twenty feet off the ground – and Kadian was smitten. He had begged me for one of his own ever since. Seven years later, I finally said yes.

Taylor was now spending the summer with us. After weeks of rain, the weather had turned warm. I recruited our friend Andy to help the boys. They would have to do most of the work, I said. Andy would only supervise, make sure everything was safe. Kadian walked down to the bottom of our garden and picked out a tall eucalyptus, a perfect tree.

We piled into Andy's white van and drove to a wood a few miles away. Andy told us that he was responsible for coppicing the hazel and beech trees here and that the owner wouldn't mind us picking a few young ones of our own, provided we paid.

We split the tasks: Andy cut trees with his chainsaw, Taylor and Kadian stripped the trees of branches and leaves, I dragged the naked poles to the van. It was hard work.

Back at the house we carried the hazel poles down to the tree. Kadian pulled himself up onto the lowest branch like a trapeze artist on his swing, upside down, legs first. He quickly climbed up, through the branches, till he was about twenty foot off the ground. 'This is where I want the platform,' he called down. 'But the ladder won't reach that far,' I shouted from below. 'That's great!' he said. 'You'll only be able to get here if you climb up. That leaves you out, old man!'

Over the next few days Kadian, Taylor and Andy set to work. They were assisted at times by Sam, and their cousins, Sipan and Kani. First, they pulled the straightest and longest of the poles up the tree with pulleys and ropes. They lashed them to the trunk at a forty-five-degree angle, in the shape of a diamond, to form the main supporting struts. Once they were good and tight, they laid the strongest and widest of the poles horizontally across these struts in a square. They then tied the remaining narrow poles, scores of them, to form a platform on which to sit.

Only once did I climb up, my legs wobbly and unsure. Kadian laughed at me as I gingerly pulled myself onto the platform, which rocked and creaked like an old ship. I am not a man with a head for heights. But the view across the valley was astonishing: before us we could see a wide lush green field filled with sheep and the houses and farm buildings across the valley. Behind us was the sharp yew-covered slope of Shoulder of Mutton, and in the far distance the long ridge of the South Downs stretched its way from Winchester in the west to Eastbourne in the east. Kadian grinned at me as if to say, 'I told you so.'

They continued to work on the tree house for the rest of the week. At times Kadian would be the busiest, scurrying around the massive tree like a monkey, working on the pulley, tying off poles, following whatever instructions Andy provided. At others, he would climb yet higher, another twenty feet above the platform, and with the others still working below, he would find a comfy spot, a Y formed between a branch and the trunk, and sit, for long periods of time, legs crossed, hand under chin, calm, happy, watching the world go by below him.

*

I would not be surprised if one day I woke up and he was back.

Where have you been? I would ask. Oh, away, he would say. I would be so glad. We would hug, and laugh, and share stories.

Soon I would be cooking him a meal, and he would be telling me some goofy joke, or teasing me about my bald head, or telling me about some gadget or other.

And I would stare at him, in love with him, loved by him, just wanting a few more seconds with my beautiful boy.

And as I write this, I hold on to him, not wanting to let him go, not wanting to feel the loss, to feel him slide from my grasp, which I know I must, and then, too soon, he's gone.

*

22 July 2012

It was a warm, lazy summer afternoon – one of those perfect days that you dream about in the middle of winter. The air was still. A few clouds slowly floated across the sky. Sam and

I were at my parents' house in Wiltshire. We were staying for the week. Sam was reading a book inside, I was dozing in the hammock.

Deb, Kadian and Taylor arrived. They had stayed an extra day at home to finish off the tree house.

'Let's go for a bike ride,' Deb said, walking up to me. 'We need some exercise.'

Half an hour later the five of us were riding down a narrow country lane away from the cottage. We cycled up and over the hill behind my parents' house, down to the A4, through Savernake Forest, where the king used to hunt his deer, to Little Bedwyn, a village with pretty red-brick cottages.

We stopped at a pub and I ordered a round of soft drinks: Diet Cokes for Sam, Deb and Taylor, lemonade and limes for Kadian and myself. I also ordered two packets of salt and vinegar crisps and two packets of cheese and onion. We all wanted the salt and vinegar crisps and were soon fighting over the last crumbs. I told them that when I was young cheese and onion crisps were in a green bag and salt and vinegar crisps were in a blue bag. For some reason they had been swapped. No one was interested.

Suddenly we heard the chimes of an ice-cream van. 'Please, Dad, please,' both children begged. Though they were thirteen and fourteen, their pleading voices were the same as when they were five and six. I looked at Deb, raising my eyebrows, asking for help. She rolled her eyes.

'No, kids,' I said, 'you don't need any more sugar.' They hustled some more. Sam giving me her best sweet-girl face and Kadian his cute-puppy look, head slightly tilted, eyes wide, overextended clownish grin. 'That's a no,' I said sharply. 'Let's get going.'

We mounted our bikes and set off. Taking a right at another

pub, we cycled past a field full of grazing sheep, and then a left at an old black-and-white iron street sign, which pointed us towards the village of Ramsbury. Kadian, Taylor and I rode in front, Sam and Deb trailed four hundred yards behind, discussing why it was that Kadian was allowed to travel to Washington the following week, and Sam had to stay at home. We began to cycle up a long, slow hill, enjoying the cooling air of the summer's evening, when Kadian sped past me with a shout of 'Later, loser!'

We cycled over the hill and down a steep slope into Ramsbury. At the bottom of the hill Taylor and I caught up with Kadian. He had stopped by a small whitewashed bridge that spanned the River Kennet. Holding up his hands to me he said, 'My hands are sore. I think my brakes are soft.' I leaned over and tried his brakes for myself; he was right, his levers moved too easily and too far. 'We have to get these fixed,' I said. 'Make sure you do that soon.'

Kadian showed me his iPhone. 'While I was waiting for you slow pokes, I recorded this.' He nodded towards a group of hairy-faced Angus cattle gathered in the field next to us. He pressed play and out came a loud mooing noise.

A few minutes later, Deb and Sam joined us at the bridge. Kadian told his mother about his weak brakes; she also ordered him to get them checked. Then, after sipping from our water bottles, and not giving the girls as much rest time as us boys, we set off for home.

Back at my parents' house we put away the bikes in the shed. In the garden we see my mother. She tells us that my aunt and uncle have invited us over for dinner later in the week. I suggest that we should ride there, taking the old Ridgeway path across the Downs. Deb will be in America by then. Sam says she'd rather drive over with her grandparents. My sister Amanda says she will come, and will bring a friend. My nephew, Taylor, says he wants to come too. Kadian adds his name to the list and says he will ask his friend Rori to join us.

I think to myself how lucky we are. And as I lock the door to the shed I look forward to another summer bike ride with my family.

*

I have a dream where Kadian stands in front of me. We are at some social gathering. We are inside. There is food and drink. He is so real, so very real. I kiss his face, again and again. He is warm, moving, alive. It feels so wonderful to touch him. He is smiling.

He tells me that he is fine. That he is happy. He tells me that it *is* going to be all right. I ask him who he is with, knowing that he cannot be happy unless he is with people, people to take care of him, people that he can take care of. But he says that he cannot tell me, that it is his 'gift', to be shared later. He does look happy, his eyes are sparkling, his cheeks are red and shiny.

I am so thankful to have even this brief time with him. I kiss him repeatedly, tears in my eyes. I know that this is a dream, I try not to wake up.

For we are together, as it should be, father and son, free from the shackles of grief.

For more information about Kadian, and the projects set up in his memory, please visit:

www.kadianharding.com

ACKNOWLEDGEMENTS

I would like to thank my family and friends for their support and love. I wouldn't have survived without you.

In particular, to the following who helped me in the writing of this book: Louise and Graham Banks, Lucy and Zam Baring, Peter Benjamin, Jez Butterworth, Mark Collins, Catherine Dawson, Daniel Glaser, Amanda Harding, Angela and Michael Harding, James and Kate Harding, Kate Harrod, Jane Hill, Gregory Kent, Farzad and Tara-Marie Mahootian, Charlie McCormick, Caitlin Morrison, Laura Quinn, Philip Selway, Julia Samuel, Gillian Tett, Dominic Valentine, Juliet Wilkinson and Amelia Wooldridge.

To those who made the Kadian memorial celebrations possible in the UK and USA: Al Blake and the staff at the Sustainability Centre in East Meon; Keith Budge, Jay Green, Joanne Greenwood and the staff and students at Bedales School; the Glenn, Levine, Lo, Mayhew, Moore, Niederhauser and Valentine families in Shepherdstown; and the crew at City Bikes for organising the ride in DC.

Thanks also to those who helped create Kadian's iTunes page: Jonathan Ive, Adam Howorth, Aubrey Ghose, David Lee and Rob Reynolds (www.kadianharding.com/apple).

For their support and help with the Kadian Mile campaign: Jason Torrance and the team at the Sustrans sustainable transport charity (www.kadianharding.com/sustrans).

For their legal support: Helen Clifford, Sally Moore, Stephen Miller, Jeremy Hyman, Jodi Sines and Martin Soames.

Thanks to Rob Hyde for permission to reproduce 'Magical People', to Dominic Valentine and Sam Harding for permission to include the lyrics to 'Beautiful Boy', and to Debora Harding, for allowing me to quote from the notebooks she kept from Kadian's infancy.

To my editor Tom Avery at William Heinemann, for his astonishing sensitivity, good humour and skill. Anna-Sophia Watts, Katherine Fry and Sally Barlow for their editorial help. Glenn O'Neill for his beautiful cover. Jason Arthur and Stephanie Sweeney, my publishers at Random House, for their encouragement. And to Gail Rebuck, for her unwavering support.

Great thanks also to my agent, Patrick Walsh, for his solidarity and love, along with the amazing team at Conville & Walsh: Henna Silvennoinen, Jake Smith-Bosanquet, Alexandra McNicoll and Carrie Plitt.

Most of all, to my daughter Sam, and wife, Debora, who have shown extraordinary courage in allowing me to write this, and whom I love beyond words.

Miss you Kads.